May You...
2020 in the yea

'20

♡

How I Survived My Son's Suicide:
Escape from Darkness

Gabrielle McLean

Please rate this Book
Amazon..com
Xulon Press

How I Survived My Son's Suicide

Escape *from* Darkness

Gabrielle Moncrease

XULON PRESS

Xulon Press
2301 Lucien Way #415
Maitland, FL 32751
407.339.4217
www.xulonpress.com

Printed in the United States of America.

ISBN-13: 978-1-5456-7857-2

Table of Contents

Introduction

This is a book the Lord impressed upon me to write, and most of the scriptures referenced here will be from the NIV[1] version of the Holy Bible. This book was written in an inspirational sort of way as the memories came; the sentences, paragraphs, and pages came together and are out of sequence. This was a process of healing for me as I wrote down these events and hopefully as you read through each page, please know this flow or style of writing wasn't meant to be confusing; it was just the process that took place.

I dedicate this book to several people—to the survivors who've attempted to take their own lives, to those who may be or are entertaining the thought of doing so, and to the friends and families who either have been or will be affected by these actions. To the survivors of attempted suicide, my hope is that after reading this, you will see things differently, realize how important your presence is here on earth, and most importantly, forgive yourself for trying to end your precious life. I hope you will change your thought processes with the understanding that what you dwell on, you will eventually act on. I hope you will get help from those who can relate to your pain. I strongly suggest a professional counselor or a strong spiritual leader who has accountability and a track record of successful outcomes with people who have experienced this type of tragedy. Please know that there is nothing to be ashamed

---

[1] . New International Version.

of. You were feeling vulnerable, weak, and hopeless. These are emotions all of us experience.

Yet I strongly warn against allowing this type of dark thinking to become a regular habit. Please don't fall into self-condemnation; forgiveness is for all who have sinned (made bad choices) and fallen short. Romans 8:1 states, "Therefore, there is now no condemnation for those who are in Christ Jesus." The most important thing for you to know is that God's grace is here for you. Simply take it and move forward "because through Christ Jesus the law of the Spirit who gives life has set you free from the law of sin and death" (Rom. 8:2). You must also forgive the people who may have caused you to carry this deep pain, ultimately further setting you free. Matthew 6:14-15 states, "For if you forgive other people when they sin against you, your heavenly Father will also forgive you. But if you do not forgive others of their sins, your Father will not forgive your sins." May God richly bless you on your journey to recovery. Keep fighting, even when you feel you can't, and wait on the Lord. He will help you and renew your strength.

> Wait on the LORD: be of good courage, and he shall strengthen thine heart: wait, I say, on the LORD. (Psalms 27:14, KJV)

To the Friends and Family of a Loved One in Need

As a family member or friend, it is reasonable to feel hurt or even angry that your loved one would even consider suicide. I have even read or heard it said that people who commit suicide are very selfish people! What's disturbing about this kind of mindset is that it lacks empathy (the ability to understand and share the feelings of another). If we have never struggled with depression, we would have no idea how hopeless it can make one feel. Once you are in a state of hopelessness, it spreads like cancer and eats away at every good possibility of a normal life. It isolates anything good from getting to you. I speak from my own experience of fighting depression for years. I didn't believe good things about myself. It wasn't until I learned how to accept me for who I was, in the unique way my Creator formed me, that I was able to resist these negative images of myself. One of the things that's on the rise is bullying. The internet is full of cruel acts enacted upon people who have been victimized by these weak-minded bullying people. They gather in groups to control others because they feel so powerless themselves. They become a negative force of unified individuals to prey on those who are not plugged into a strong group of positive people. So, friends, family members, be a solution to the problem, not the problem itself. Even if you don't understand the negative cycle your loved one has fallen into, don't minimize it and don't escalate it either. First pray for wisdom. Then trust that the Lord will guide you to the most sensible way to help your loved one.

If any of you lack wisdom, let him ask of God, that giveth to all men liberally, and upbraideth not, and it shall be given him. (James 1:5, KJV)

If you are reading this too late because the tragedy has become final and your loved one is gone, please don't beat yourself up with the "blame game." If you didn't handle things as well as you would have liked with your loved one, it will do you no good whatsoever to blame yourself and live a life of regret. That doesn't help anyone. You are human, and as the quote goes, "To err is human." Do not condemn yourself. It's important to get good counseling during this time. There are good counselors and bad counselors out there. Trust your instincts in choosing one. If something doesn't feel right, don't continue to go. Your inner voice is usually right. Keep searching for an advisor who has the proper training and understanding of what you are dealing with. There is a bright side, and that is you can know once you've taken steps toward healing, you can begin to help others to not follow in the footsteps of your error. See the signs and become proactive when it comes to your loved ones. Do not condemn yourself. It's important to get good counseling during this time. There are good counselors and bad counselors out there. Trust your instincts in choosing a counselor. If something doesn't feel right, don't continue to go. Your inner voice is usually right. Keep searching for an advisor who has the proper training and understanding for what you are dealing with.

To My Special Friends and Family

Thanks to my eldest son, Genesis, for handling the very difficult arrangements for Reese's memorial services and for being a great big brother, as well as a fine father to his children and a great son to me. I know my grandchildren will miss the playfulness of their uncle Reese. May God strengthen and keep you all, Faraji, Amire, Kamil, Nasreen, and Anya. Another heartfelt thank you, Genesis. It's because of you I met Mona, who danced so beautifully at the memorial service. Thanks to Pastor Ervin and Stephanie for sharing your visions with us and supporting us all the way. Thanks Carlos and Patrick (Peanut) for being at the hospital. You were like guardian angels, and we love you. To Angelia and Sierra, my heart goes out to you both for your loss of a partner and father. To my sister Joy, who prayed with me all night on night number three. Thanks to my former pastor Raymond McIntosh for speaking at my son's memorial service here in Las Vegas. Thanks, Dominique, my childhood buddy, for singing so beautifully. Also, a shout-out to Lisa in Spokane for singing the song I requested, "My Joy." There are so many people who helped make this transition so much smoother. Pastor J. Jones and his wife and family; Ms. Vita; my brother James Randall; Dennis Mitchell and Terry; my atomic prayer partner Stephanie. Additionally, a shout-out to my new friend Donnell Holliday: thanks for the research on the effects of drugs. Your contribution was tremendous. I wish you much success in your medical career. Thank you to Jonathan Sifuentes, who helped with last-minute editing and formatting issues. Thank you so much, Joy and Krystal, for your creative touch on the drawing of Frank at such short notice. I wish the best for you both in your careers.

To my very best friend, Willetta Cody, who always believed in me and has showed me unconditional love since my young adult years. She is definitely my sister from another family. You are an angel.

To my spiritual mom Marion and Toni Parsi, to TCPW, aka "The Prayer Hogs" prayer group, our morning conference call sisters Carol, Tina, Maria, Tiffany, Gilda, Sandy, brothers Benny, Robert, and Terry, and Willetta's sisters Erma, Dorothy, Debra, and daughter Yuvonka, and Noel—love you guys.

To Gloria and the prayer warriors Carol, Shirley, Tina, Gay, Mark, and Brenda at The House of Prayer in Henderson, Nevada. To my prayer partners at my church at East Vegas Christian Center: Cathy, Warren, Jody, and Yordany. Thanks to Pastors Troy and Sandra for their leadership and covering.

Each one of you has been a tremendous support, and I am grateful for your involvement in this matter.

Chapter 1

The Good Samaritan

Helping Others through Trauma

The story of the Good Samaritan comes to mind when I think back on that early morning I received the news my youngest son had been seriously injured. Luke 10:25-37 is where the story is found in the Bible. It's a story about a man who got robbed, stripped, and then beaten almost to the point of death. A traveling priest noticed the beaten man barely breathing alongside the road, but instead of stopping to assist the man, he crossed the street and continued his journey. Then another man who was a Levite did the same thing. But the third man, who was the Good Samaritan, was the one who showed him compassion. He bandaged the man's wounds then put him on his horse or donkey and brought him to a lodge where he took care of him. The next day, he gave money to the lodge innkeeper and asked him to keep an eye on the man and told him if the amount he gave him didn't cover the expenses, he would make up the difference when he returned.

My story is a little different. The morning I received the numerous phone calls and text messages telling me my youngest child was in dire straits, many people showed compassion and sent prayers, but one person in particular showed great compassion. Vita was an old childhood acquaintance that I had recently been reunited with by a mutual friend, Joyce. Unfortunately, Vita understood what I was dealing with because her youngest son died tragically some years ago. She walked me through all the necessary things I should do and was such a big help to me at the time because I felt trapped inside my own skin. I needed someone to tell me what to do. My energy levels where depleted, and without step-by-step guidance, it would have been just too difficult to bear.

It's usually the people who have experienced great opposition and tragedy who respond the quickest to a need such as mine or that of the man who was robbed in the Bible.

Compassion

We live in a world that is so fast-paced that people hardly speak to one another. We rely so heavily on texting and emailing that we are losing our verbal communication skills. Although it's a quick and easy way to keep in touch, we have become unbalanced and less sensitive to other people's needs to the point where if someone offers us assistance, we are surprised and often suspicious of their motives. Yet it should be the norm according to Scripture. Genesis 4:9-16 tells us that we are our brother's keeper. We are not supposed to abuse or neglect one another. Jesus showed us great compassion all through the Scriptures. He gave us a great footprint to follow. Compassion is the ability to feel what another person is going through and not wanting that person to suffer. I believe the rough storms you've encountered in your life were meant to help you gain strength in your weakness and to show you how to teach others how to ride the waves. If you know someone who is facing a difficult situation, ask yourself how you would feel if you were in that same situation and what you would like someone to do for you. If you practice by asking the Holy Spirit for guidance, you will learn how to become a Good Samaritan. We can't help everyone; it's not humanly possible. But with the counsel from above, we can be sure that what we are meant to do will unfold before us as it should.

This chapter is so important because when trauma strikes, people aren't prepared. It's a surprise and a shock. When you are in a shocked state of mind, you may look and even act normal, but you're not. You are disconnected from your true feelings. So, remember, when helping someone who is grieving or in great pain, give firm direction but with as much compassion and sensitivity as possible.

Chapter 2

Dreams and Visions

A dream is defined as "a series of thoughts, images, sensations, and emotions occurring involuntarily in a person's mind during certain stages of sleep."[1] I have heard many theories or opinions on why we dream. Some say we dream only when we eat certain foods within a short time of going to bed; others say we dream only when we are going through deep emotional pain or stress. Some people claim to have the gift of interpreting dreams. The mention of dreams dates back thousands of years to about 3000–5000 BC in Mesopotamia. Dream interpreters would write on clay tables what they believed the dream meant. The Greeks believed that dreams were messages from certain deities and the deceased and predicted one's future. Sigmund Freud, who developed a discipline of psychoanalysis, wrote much on dream theories and their interpretations. He believed dreams were manifestations of our deepest desires and anxieties often linked to childhood memories. The average length of time a dream lasts is a few seconds to thirty minutes. If a person wakes up during the dream, they will most likely remember it. Most people dream three to five times in one night on average.

The Bible and Dreams

In biblical history, the first mention of dreams is found in Genesis 20:1-7: a story about Abraham and his wife, Sarah. Abraham was considered a very blessed man because of the tremendous favor he had with God. The Lord promised to make him "father of many nations." He was also very wealthy and married to what we would today call a hottie (she was gorgeous). It's true he was blessed to have such a beautiful spouse, but it also caused him great anxiety. For instance, in the presence of King Abimelech, he told a little white lie. He said that Sarah was his sister, which was partly true but he left out a few details. She was his half-sister, but most importantly, she was his rib, aka wife. Of course, in today's times that would be considered incest. This certainly can be researched further, but in my search for answers I concluded that there were no laws at that time against such an action, and because the Ten Commandments were written hundreds of years later, at that time it was legal to wed relatives.

A Warning to the King

When the king laid eyes upon Sarah, he wanted her for himself. Now you see the reason for Abraham's cover story. He didn't want the king to kill him and take his wife. This could have possibly become a harsh reality, so he got scared and lied and told the king she was his sister. The king swooped right in and took her from him and added her to his harem. But when the king fell asleep, the Lord appeared to him and warned him to not lay a finger on Sarah because she was Abraham's wife. He told the king that if he disobeyed, he would lose his life and his whole family would join him in the family *mastaba*[2] extremely early. So the outcome, of course, was in Abraham and Sarah's favor. This would be classified as a warning dream.

---

[2] . An ancient Egyptian tomb with a rectangular base, sloping sides, and a flat roof.

Types of Dreams

Warning dream: The type I just mentioned. See the example above with Abraham and Sarah where God appeared to the king.

Revealing dream: In the warning dream that God gave King Abimelech, there was some revelation or revealing going on because Abraham hid the truth about being married to Sarah, and God uncovered it in a dream. But in Genesis chapter 37, the story shows or reveals something to Joseph. Joseph's father favored him more than his other siblings because he had him in his old age, and his siblings despised him because of that. In Joseph's dream, God revealed to him what was going to take place in the future—he would become great someday. His jealous brothers already disliked him and were even more upset when he told them about his dream and how God told him he would be famous and rule over them one day. They conspired in their jealous rage to silence him by faking his death then sold him into slavery. But Joseph, after suffering that fate and much more devastation, clung tightly to the promise God made him, and the Dream became reality. Sometime afterward, he was given a new name: Zaphenath-Paneah; this name was given to him because of his ability to reveal secrets. After the name change, he got promoted to governor.

Impartation dream: In 1 Kings 3:5-12, the Lord appeared to Solomon in a dream and asked him what he wanted. Solomon could have been greedy and asked for riches, but instead he asked for the wisdom to be a great king. In the dream, God appeared well pleased by this and granted him his request, plus a lot of extra things, including an extreme amount of wealth and power he never asked for.

Strategy dream: The book of Judges chapters 6 and 7 contain the story of Gideon and how an angel appeared to him in a dream and revealed the plan God had to overtake the Midianite army with just a few men. Later, a Midianite soldier told of a dream he had that revealed to him that Gideon's army would win the fight even though the Midianite soldiers outnumbered Gideon's army.

Visions

Promise dream: In Genesis 15, God told Abram (his name before God changed it to Abraham) in a vision that He would bless him with a son. It didn't seem as though he and Sarah would ever have a child of their own because they were getting older, but God gave them instructions to follow and spoke to them of many great things to come.

Future dream: In Joel chapters 1-3, Joel's vision is of the future. He tells others about the visions and warns that people need to take heed of what lies ahead. He tells them it's going to be a scary time upon the earth and there will be many signs that the Lord is coming to earth, but before His return, He would fill His people with His presence and purpose. People will see many supernatural events take place, and it shall be a great day for some and not such a great day for those who didn't take heed of the warnings.

God's Glory and future events: Revelation 3 talks about John's vision of angels. He sees a door open in heaven, and he hears a voice like a trumpet telling him to come up higher and that much will be revealed. In his vision, there are beautiful jewels, gold crowns, and different sorts of heavenly creatures. My favorite part of this vision is the angels repeatedly saying, "Holy, holy, holy is the Lord God Almighty who was and is to come."

God speaks to us in different ways. Be aware of when He is trying to get your attention. Open yourself up to the Holy Spirit because God is real. If you believe in Him and know the Word of God is true and that the events I've shared are written in the Bible, then you will see that God is still the same God today as He was back then and He still speaks through dreams and visions. Has He been trying to get your attention in a dream or vision?

There were many times my mind would visualize my son being in a wheelchair, and I would resist the vision because it was so unpleasant. I didn't know in detail what it meant when I saw it, but I believe because I saw it years prior that somehow, even though it was one of my most difficult experiences, it subconsciously helped prepare my heart for this tragedy. My son knew he made a mistake when his spirit began to float away from his body, but by then it was too late to undo what had been done. He saw his helpless body that had been damaged by the bullet to his brain and knew he would have to go through multiple therapies to recover. So in God's mercy, He honored my son's wishes and didn't allow him to return to his damaged shell. I know that sometimes our minds may wander and imagine things because that's being human, but if you pray and ask the Lord to help you understand your dreams or visions, He will respond.

The Lord wants to give His children good things. The heavenly Father gives good gifts to those who ask. Matthew 7:11 (NLT) states, "So if you sinful people know how to give good gifts to your children, how much more will your heavenly Father give good gifts to those who ask Him?" Dreams and visions are prophetic gifts. Romans 12:6 tells us we each have gifts that differ according to the grace that is given to us. Romans 12:3 declares that every one of us has a measure of faith, meaning some simply believe more than others or trust what God is telling them more than others, and if you have little faith, you can ask for more and He will increase that.

Visions of Hope

> Where there is no vision, the people perish: but he that keepeth the
> law, happy is he.   (Proverbs 29:18, KJV)

Dreams and visions go hand in hand. They are pictures that lead us to a place of enlightenment. Without mental pictures of hope to guide us through life, we would shrink back and doubt what lies ahead. Visions bring us confidence; answers are hidden within them. They will lead and guide us to a place beyond complacency if we choose. That's why it's so important to pay close attention to them. In many cases, the Holy Spirit will use them to get our attention. In this instance of my child being wounded from the decision to end his precious life, I needed to see a different picture, such as a vision of hope, because what I was about to embark upon was a journey that would have stolen all the hope and confidence that I had in the wonderful plans that God had for me and my children.

Holy Visitation

It was a quarter past midnight, and my prayer partner, Jodie, and I had just completed an hour of prayer. As we entered into the second hour of the prayer, I began to feel tired and told her it was time for me to go to bed. But before I hung the phone up, I saw an image of something hovering over my bed. It looked like a great white owl, and it had something hanging from its beak. I told Jodie about it, and she asked me what it was holding. I told her it looked like a white piece of cloth, like a bandage. Right after explaining this vision to her, I grew very sleepy. I felt very depleted, not only from my demanding work schedule but also from my other responsibilities, including the forty-nine-hour monthly prayer regimen. The Lord had assigned me to pray three or four times daily, and it left me drained by the end of each day (yes, prayer is work).

A few hours after, I had the vision of the owl hovering over my bed (in Hebrew culture, an owl is a sign of death and devastation; they hoot and cry and are birds of prey[2]). At about 1:30 a.m., I had two phone calls from Genesis (my eldest son) and thought maybe one of my grandchildren had gotten hold of the phone. It was a restless night, and I kept falling in and out of sleep. I woke up again and checked my phone about an hour later, and this time, I had forty phone calls. I knew whatever had happened was serious. I sprung out of bed and called my eldest son's father because we had numerous talks in the past regarding how we would handle a desperate situation such as this one. Buddy answered the phone, and with his voice broken and full of emotion, he started to cry. So I hung up and began to pace the floor, dreading having to call him back but knowing I had to. I slowly dialed his number again, but this time, I spoke as soon as he answered. "Buddy, listen to me! Please answer this question first! Are both of my sons alive? Then you can tell me anything else if you want to." He tried hard to stop his sobbing, and in a mumbled, shaky tone, he uttered the words I needed to hear. "Both of your sons are alive." Then I gave him permission to give me the rest of the details.

He told me Reese, my youngest son, shot himself in the head and that the doctors said he had a small chance of survival. He said we should pray that his brain doesn't swell because if it does, they won't be able to go inside his skull to repair the damage. I restrained from crying so I could hear every detail, then when all was said, I hung up the phone and ran down the stairs to confront the Holy Spirit. My tears were running down my face like a water faucet. I held my hands out wide and screamed, "Why? Why? Why?" And the Holy Spirit appeared right before me with His arms stretched out even wider and said, "Because he doesn't want to be here anymore!"

Seeing Jesus standing in front of me was powerful! His hands were stretched out wide to illustrate that He had done everything He could to protect my child, and in a flash my mind raced back to all of the times the Lord would awaken me in the late hours and early morning to pray a shield of protection over my children and how days later it would be revealed how Reese had gotten in an accident and came out with little or no injuries. Once when I was on vacation visiting my family, I got news that Reese had been in a bad motorcycle wreck and his bike was totaled. Reese's godmother, Willetta, and I rushed to the hospital in time to hear the doctor tell my son how blessed and lucky he was to walk away from such a tragic accident with no injuries. All of these memories flashed through my mind at once.

Living Water

There I was again, standing in the middle of my living room, ready and waiting to confront the Holy Spirit. The thought of losing one of my sons was too much for me to bear, especially with the amount of time I spent in prayer for them. It was too hard to accept this sort of news. The Lord very quickly disappeared. In a loud and desperate voice, I yelled, "I'm going to lose my mind right now!" But before my body hit the floor, a loud voice that spoke directly to my spirit belted, "Get into the spirit so you can see what I am doing." Everything from that point on was in slow motion. I saw a river of pure, clear water right before me in my living room, and the scriptures came to mind, how living water was very much a part of how God revealed Himself to man. As a matter of fact, years earlier, I experienced an open vision of heaven. In this vision, before me was a pool of clear water that was alive like the scriptures (read in John 4:10 and 7:38), but in my vision, it was made clear that this water was alive and capable of worshiping God because I saw each drop of water singing songs of praise and honor to The Most High God in different genres! It was such a miracle that had I not witnessed it, I would have never dreamed such a thing existed in heaven.

I looked at the water and saw my son's soul traveling fast toward red and gold flames of fire that were coming from a deep, dark place below. I could hear the crackling of the fire. Then I saw a large hand, and I knew it was God's hand. It appeared in the clouds like a baseball catcher's mitt. God's hand reached down and caught my son's soul as it was headed toward the hot flames. My son's soul was now safe in the palm of a mighty, omnipotent power. Suddenly I was face to face with the Holy Spirit once again and watched God's hand touch His chest. He said, "He's with Me." God's Voice was like another scripture I had read, Revelation 14:2: God's voice is so powerful like rushing waters and thunder. Hearing those words, my tears began to flow. All this happened in just a matter of minutes or seconds, but it seemed like hours. I lay there weeping on the floor of my living room because the pain was so great. But then I rose up with tears still streaming down my face and rejoiced in the gratitude that my son was with the Lord. That's all I ever wanted and all I ever prayed for, besides keeping them (Reese and Genesis) safe from harm's way.

Pulling It All Together

I was in a supernatural daze. Something was happening to me, and it completely took over. I looked like myself, but that spiritual part of me was in control; I was really somewhere else. It reminded me of the famous painting of footprints in the sand because Jesus was definitely carrying me through all of my pain and sorrows. My friend Vita called and gave me directions to follow. This was all part of the supernatural place I was in. People would just show up and drive me places and do things for me, and all I had to do was show up. The Word of God was pouring out of my spirit like a fountain. I remained in a place of worship, and that was my strength.

When you get this kind of news, your only way out to sanity is to surrender your total self to the Holy Spirit. Satan's plan was for me to fall down on that floor and get up a mindless, hopeless mom, but because of the prayers of the righteous, and God's mercy and grace and His loving kindness, I was able to withstand one of the worst days of my life and still have victory.

Chapter 3

Keeping Your Head Above Water

Confirmation

During this time, many of my friends, clergy, and family had visions to assure me that this was all real. Sister Gloria Sweney, CEO of The House of Prayer in Henderson, Nevada, called me and confirmed that my son was with Jesus. She said she saw him walking with Jesus in a vision. My son Reese was involved in the secular music industry. He opened shows for Grammy performers for several years and also produced music for many artists. His main influence was a producer named Ervin who at the time was living a wicked life of sin but had a great deal to do with the development of my son's music career.

After Reese's death, there were many questions concerning what might have led up to this event. Ervin talked about how he had left the music scene for a while to answer the call that God had on his life, and during that time, my son had probably gotten involved with other people. Ervin was not aware of all the things that had led to my son's tragedy. Around the time that Ervin heard the news of what happened to Reese (his former artist), he and his wife, Stephanie, immediately went to the hospital to be by his side for moral and spiritual support. They told me they were around the bed and heard him take his last voluntary breath. They saw his spirit leave his body and walk around the bed to see for the first time the damage he had done to himself. Incredibly, then they witnessed Jesus appear right alongside him asking if he wanted to go back inside his body. He replied, "No," and walked away with Jesus. Here is a demonstration of God's mercy. He could have told my son to go back into his body that my son chose to destroy, but instead he allowed him to go with him to a place of green pastures and peace. It was the Lord's choice how to handle what happened with my son. He was there for Reese with His mercy and grace, as I'm sure He's been for others who were hurting and made the decision to end their valuable lives. However, this doesn't give people a license or an excuse to take their own lives because no one knows the outcome of that decision except God.

Negative Thoughts Lead to Depression

Depression is something that's familiar to most of us. It is important to know, however, that it can be controlled. You have to think healthy. Just as your body can't be healthy and build muscle and sustain your energy if all you eat is junk food, your mind can't be healthy unless it too is fed positive thoughts. What you dwell on is what you will become. Dwelling in unforgiveness, for example, is toxic and will destroy your future. We must forgive. It is a commandment because salvation was built on forgiveness. Matthew 6:15 states, "But if you do not forgive others their sins, your Father will not forgive your sins." God gave His Son for as a sacrifice for us to be delivered from sin, and Jesus loved His Father and us so much, He died so we can live. There is no way around the fact that we must forgive and move on. Unforgiveness is like cancer. It eats away everything that is good. If you are dwelling on negative thoughts or reliving the awful things people did to you and rehearsing them like a play, just stop doing it! Gain control of your thoughts. I am aware that there are chemical imbalances that can bring your mood to an all-time low, and I know the feelings are real and some of you even experience physical pain, but as a person who has had plenty of practice fighting these demons, I offer you the way I survive these emotions (because I still fight depression) and hope that they will aid you in your journey to victory.

Beware of the Sharks

When I think of sharks, the first thing that comes to my mind is the movie *Jaws*. I think of people running scared trying to clear out of the water before they get eaten alive. Sometimes I feel like I'm inside a shark tank, especially when I'm in situations that make me feel uncomfortable. Sometimes being with the wrong crowd of people can make you feel like someone's lunch, especially if you're a guppy trying to hang with the predators. God made us all different, and we are all special in some way or another. You must learn this about yourself and be aware of when you are in over your head.

Some of the people in your life are not meant for you to become best friends with because they don't have your best interests in mind. When we carry a relationship to a deeper level that hasn't been tried or tested to see if this person can be trusted, we end up getting eaten alive by these people who have aggressive personalities, and we begin to doubt who we are because we are now comparing ourselves to these shark-like personality types. Please know I am not putting down aggressive people. It takes all kinds of people to make the world go around. But there are destructive people in the world that are a bad influence, so you should beware. If you are a sensitive person and the people you hang around are not sensitive, you are in a zone which you are not equipped to handle. You know you feel uncomfortable, but you won't give in to the warning signs. This will become an unwise decision for you because it will cloud your judgment when other warning signs occur. Then you become numb to your true feelings, and this can cause depression, something you must try to avoid at all costs.

Be true to yourself, know your value, and never compare yourself to others to measure your self-worth for any relationship because the people who love and care about you would never want you to do that. The Bible talks about brotherly love and how friends should respect and love one another. The principles in the Bible are a solid foundation for you to build upon when emotions run high. You will need good, firm advice to draw from. The oldest and bestselling book of all time, regardless of trends, is still the Bible.

Proverbs 1:8-19 talks about listening to solid and wise counsel from your parents (you can also apply this to people who care about your well-being) and living according to the Scriptures. It will save you a lot of heartache and pain if you listen and obey them. It also talks about those shark-like people who will lead you into destruction if you follow them. Wise counsel comes from wise people. Make sure the people you take counsel from are demonstrating what they teach. Not everyone comes from a Christian background or even a stable background. In fact, this could be one of the reasons why people fall into bad situations. Proverbs 13:20 states, "Walk with the wise and become wise, for a companion of fools suffers harm." The book of Proverbs is full of wisdom, and believe me, it takes wisdom to keep a healthy, balanced lifestyle. Read it often. I also suggest you find a good Bible study group and invest in Bible commentaries to help you understand what you're reading. Keep in mind, the more you read and study the Word of the Lord, the more understanding you will gain, and that will lead to more revelations. Revelations will come when you take the time to learn and meditate on His Word.

My Own Battle with Depression

I already mentioned that what you dwell on will probably occur. That's why I spend a lot of my time praying, reading God's Word, or spending time in worship. According to Scripture, we are renewed in our minds, and it's a process. Romans 12:2 says, "Do not conform to the pattern of this world, but be transformed by the renewing of your mind. Then you will be able to test and approve what God's will is—His good, pleasing and perfect will." Philippians 4:8 is another good verse you can read regarding this subject. I have always struggled with instant gratification (this is part of the struggle of depression). I wanted the end results yesterday.

Thank God for the teachers in my life who hung in there with me and didn't give up. They brought accountability to my life and helped me stay focused and on track. It's unfortunate that in my family, there is a history of personality disorders. To keep things on the light side, I would often joke about mental illness in my family so that it wouldn't have power over me. This has been an effective way for me to sift out the bad feelings of shame and disgust that I felt about being born into my family. I say this not to blame them but to free myself from any bondage. None of us have any say in who our parents are going to be or who our other family members are going to be. Making the best out of whatever you were born into is what you must learn, so you can achieve and fulfill your purpose, because we all certainly have one.

Chapter 4

Hallmark from Heaven

I still like to show my appreciation the old-fashioned way, in a special card with just the right message. Today's culture is full of instant ways to express gratitude or recognition. Through the internet we can send each other cute little cartoons that sing or dance or play instruments. Last year, for Christmas I received an animated short story about Christmas and an e-card with falling snow and a clickable lantern that made the whole scene light up—the trees in the yard and the lights in the house. It was so beautiful I played it over and over. It was great! But I always felt there was something special about a Hallmark card.

The Hallmark card I received was really more like a hologram, and like a hologram, it was much more splendid because it was really my son, the more improved version. He was so different. He had nothing to hide and no reason to be ashamed. He had no sorrow or pain. He was honest, direct, awesome, and perfect. I call this visitation my Hallmark from heaven because the message was so regal. It was a message straight from heaven from the best creator of all, the one and only, His Majesty!

I was sitting at my desk finishing an assignment for a class, and I suddenly began to feel sad. I was thinking this would be my first birthday without hearing from my youngest son. He would call early every year. Not able to concentrate on my schoolwork, I shut down my computer and shoved the workbook that was on my desk away from me. The heaviness of loss was upon me, and the reality that Genesis and I would never lay eyes on Reese again was a thought that I was trying hard not to dwell upon.

Is This Real?

It was 11:50 p.m., just before midnight. I felt the hairs on my neck and arms stand straight up. I saw my son Reese appear right in front of me. I was so stunned I couldn't move. I was in such shock and disbelief that this was happening. I called out to God with everything within me and asked Him what all this meant. Was I going crazy? Or was there some evil witch somewhere casting a spell to scare me witless? I waited patiently for an answer, and finally, one came. I looked to the right of me and saw an image of an angel and then felt a calming peace overtake me and a soft voice tell me to just sit back and relax. After seeing the angel and hearing the familiar voice of God, I knew I was in safe company. From some of the passages I've read in the Bible, I knew it was God because the angel was on my right hand. Isaiah 41:13 states, "For I am the Lord your God, who takes hold of your right hand and says to you, do not fear I will help you." Psalms 73:23 (NASB) says, "Nevertheless I am continually with you; you have taken hold of my right hand." Whatever was about to happened was divinely orchestrated from heaven. I took a deep breath, and after that, it was as if God had a remote control and He had pushed the start button. My son put his hand on my left shoulder and began to speak.

"Mom, I see everything you're doing! You're going to make it! Just never give up and keep going! You're going to do great!" I was so scared but excited and overwhelmed, so I jumped up and ran inside my open closet in my bedroom to escape my confused emotions of ecstasy and terror. Inside my closet was the outfit I had chosen to wear for my birthday. Staring at the dress hanging there, I wondered if I had entered the Twilight Zone or something. It was wonderful but scary. My heart was racing, and the hairs everywhere on my body were at full attention. And here I was, hiding inside my closet from a spirit that can walk through walls. I shook my head and tried to think about how I was going to accessorize my birthday outfit.

About that time, I heard my son's voice again, and I slowly turned to face his voice. He was standing inside the entrance to my walk-in closet, and he conversed with me, just like old times. He looked at me and said, "Mom, wear that dress for your birthday," which was the dress I had already picked out for my birthday! Then he said, "Mom, wear the shoes that match it," and I thought, *Do I have shoes to match this?* You see, Reese and I loved fashion, and we would buy each other clothes. His closet and man cave looked like a department store, and if I had more room in my house, mine probably would look like one also. As I stood in the middle of my closet trying to grasp what was going on with this incredible visit from heaven, I began to read the labels on the boxes of shoes and saw the one labeled "leopard heels." They were there, just like he said. I had actually forgotten about them. As I lowered the box from the shelf, I looked at him again, and he said, "I'm sorry I hurt you, and tell Aunt Netta [his godmother] I said hello." Then he said, "I have to go now." And he was gone in a flash.

I was shocked and kept wondering if that just really happened. It was so amazing and left such an impression on me that I walked around in a daze for about a week.

Boundaries Are God's Protection

It really isn't rocket science, as some may think. God has His Word to inform us of what is spiritually safe and what isn't. After sharing this story with several people, there was some skepticism about my testimony being biblically sound. Thanks to that challenge, I decided to research it for myself, and here is what I found. In the story of King Saul (1 Samuel 28), he wasn't hearing the voice of God speak to him anymore, and he was afraid and concerned. He wanted to hear from God what was going to occur in the near future. First, let me say that God speaks to us when He is ready. We must never try to force God for an answer, but we can certainly be desperate to ask. He took the wrong approach. He consulted a witch to conjure up the prophet Samuel's spirit so he could get some answers. That is against the laws of the Scriptures, which makes it spiritually illegal. Leviticus 19:31 states, "Do not turn to mediums or seek out spiritists, for you will be defiled by them. I am the Lord your God." These things are forbidden by God for our protection against evil spirits that would make havoc in our lives if we open this supernatural door.

The difference between my experience and King Saul's is that he purposely consulted a witch or medium, who probably led him in deception to a demon spirit instead of the prophet Samuel. Or perhaps he really did speak to Samuel, but the way he was conjured up wasn't God's way of doing things. I didn't ask to speak to my son; it was something God wanted to show me to help encourage me and ease my pain. The Lord is who He is and can do as He pleases, but He won't stray from His written Word because His Word lays a safe foundation for us to follow so we don't get ourselves in trouble. Deuteronomy 18:10-13 goes into more detail about how you shouldn't consult witches or wizards to raise the dead to talk to them (necromancy).

The Outpouring

We live in a world where people want more than just what they see on the surface; people want the supernatural. That's because we were really created to live with supernatural powers, but sin got in the way. Supernatural powers become perverted or illegal if they are not gained from the authority of the Holy Spirit.

In the last days, God says, I will pour out my Spirit on all people, your sons and daughters shall prophesy, your young men will see visions, your old men will dream dreams. (Acts 2:17)

24

But you will receive power when the Holy Spirit comes on you and
you will be my witnesses in Jerusalem and in all Judea and Samaria
and to the ends of the earth.   (Acts 1:8)

This outpouring can only come to those who are believers in God
the Father, Jesus the Son, and the Holy Spirit.

We must not be ashamed to claim Him in His entirety. God wants
to demonstrate His power through all of us. He created us to be His
witnesses. I do realize that thinking about the supernatural may be a bit
scary for some, but it is as real as the air you breathe. You can't see it, but
it's all around us every day, supplying us with what we need to survive.
The air that exists all around us is invisible, and yet we never doubt it's
our life source. You can talk to God anytime; just open your heart and
mind and test the waters.

My stepfather didn't believe in God at all, but the minute he was in
a deep, dark place where he could find no peace, he decided to take his
chance on the God that seemed to have changed his daughter's life. It's
really simple—just believe He is Lord and ask Him into your heart. You
may remember hearing this verse if you attended Sunday school: "If you
confess with your mouth the Lord Jesus and believe in your heart that
God raised Him from the dead, you shall be saved" (Rom. 10:9, NKJV).
Isn't that easy? The real work then begins through you. You must plug
into a good Bible-based church with Bible studies and classes so you
can learn how to live your new life. At church, you will find people
from all walks of life. You will meet new Christians and those that were
seemingly born with a Bible in their hand. But don't become discouraged, because God chooses whom He wants. If you just accepted Christ,
you must move forward and let nothing stop your spiritual journey.
Remember, if you've attempted suicide and you were unsuccessful, you
have great work ahead of you to help save others from making the mistake of ending what God wanted to continue.

The Origin of Evil

Wikipedia defines evil as "something morally bad or wicked. It is the opposite of good...an action that hurts people or breaks certain rules..."[3] (here is my example of very important written rules such as the Ten Commandments [God's law]). The Ten Commandments are in Exodus 20. The origin of evil is a lengthy story, but I will explain it as briefly as possible. Lucifer was an angel that God made—the worshiping angel who became Satan, aka the devil, after the fall. Isaiah 14:12-14 talks about the fallen one from heaven called Lucifer. He was an anointed angel of God—a chosen one. After the fall, he was known as a king in Babylon. Also read Ezekiel 28:11-19: how Lucifer, aka Satan, was created so perfectly, then pride took over his heart. In a nutshell, this story explains how evil occurred: it was through pride and arrogance that he believed he was God or that he could replace God and he began to want worship for himself. The example of him being king demonstrates how evil works when you become full of pride; because you have extraordinary looks, gifts, or talent, you become like Satan and want worship. Your heart becomes full of pride, which separates you from the one who created you in this divine way in the first place; and then you fall. But he became full of pride and began behaving badly and plotted to take over heaven.

This was unacceptable to God, so Satan was evicted from heaven, along with a third of the angels who plotted with him. Since Satan's plan to take over heaven was unsuccessful, he chose to try to control God's precious children that God created in His image and likeness. Adam and Eve were the first humans on earth, so Satan began there by tempting Eve in the garden to disobey God. Adam and Eve yielded to the temptation, and all humans have wrestled with good and evil ever since. But the more you obey God's commandments, the easier it becomes to do what's right. You must practice God's commandments to become successful

---

[3]   Evil." Wikipedia: The Free Encyclopedia. 2019. https://simple.wikipedia.org/w/index. php?title=Evil&oldid=6251430.

at this. I encourage you to study the Bible so you can live a successful life. Please read Ezekiel 28:13-19. This scripture goes into further detail about who Satan is, how he was once good but turned evil.

Chapter 5

Following Instructions

I have noticed in my lifetime that following instructions is not always easy and is usually tedious and taxing. When you buy something that needs to be assembled, it usually comes with an instruction booklet or a sheet of instructions. I don't know about you, but if an item has more than four steps to put it together, my next step is to ball up the paper and aim for the garbage. I don't like doing anything that needs too much figuring out. I blame this on Roza (my mom) because she gave me too many puzzles when I was a child. The only way I could go out to play was to either read a book or put together a puzzle. Most of the time, I chose to read a book because it was easier for me. As humans, we tend to go for what's less of a headache or hassle. There are some that like a challenge, but I think the majority of us tend toward easy street. I don't have a problem following directions at work or at church, but I really dislike gadget instructions. I've thrown away the instructions many times after the fourth step and then ended up putting things together backwards or upside down. It's those experiences that have taught me that no matter how many steps it takes to put something together correctly, it's well worth it in the end to follow the instructions. Even though it might be difficult and taxing to do, if it's put together right, you can use it for years to come and enjoy it. That's the benefit of following instructions.

Following God's Instructions

There are many passages in the Bible regarding God's instructions. In Proverbs 19:20 (ESV), we're told, "Listen to advice and accept instruction, that you may gain wisdom in the future." Psalms 32:8 (ESV) states, "I will instruct you and teach you in the way you should go; I will counsel you with my eye upon you." And Proverbs 12:1 (ESV) says, "Whoever loves discipline loves knowledge, but he who hates reproof is stupid." That last one was pretty strong! It tells us we're just plain stupid if we're not willing to discipline ourselves to gain the knowledge to get us to the next level in life. There is one more scripture I would like you to look up. It's Proverbs 8:32-36, and it explains that you obtain the favor of God when you hear and obey God's instructions.

Following God's Instructions: The Pricey Payoff

I want to share with you how God prepared me for the tragic mistake my son made on January 19th, 2013, between the hours of midnight and 2:30 a.m. Most people have heard of prayer and understand its purpose; therefore, many of us pray. But the call to pray is a little different. It's called intercessory prayer. The Bible declares that many are called but few are chosen. What this means simply is God needs people He can trust and use that are available to do what's required. There are many jobs available in His kingdom, but in this case, I'm talking about prayer. Intercessory prayer requires discipline because if you get sleepy after five minutes of praying and fall asleep, that won't get the job done. I don't know how other intercessors (sometimes called watchmen) started their prayer journey, but I can share how I became a watchman. In the beginning of my walk with God, He told me to specifically pray for others. Everything in life has a price, even if you were told it's free. We're even told salvation is free, but is it if a Savior had to die for us? Jesus paid the price with His life to set us free. He is the only one who could pay such a price because He has the power and authority from above to do so.

I worked the same job for years. I didn't have to rise early for work because my shift began at 10 a.m., so I would get up between 7 a.m. and 8 a.m. five days a week. It was very easy. But on November 12th, 2012, around 6:30 p.m., my life was changed in ways I never imagined it could be. I was sitting in a chair in my bedroom reading a book, and the Holy Spirit began to send me specific instructions. He was talking so fast I could barely keep up. I sat up quickly and grabbed a pen and paper and wrote down every word. "You will pray for seven months, seven days a week, and each month you will fast for seven days. You will pray for forty-nine hours each month." I was baffled, not because He gave me instructions to pray, but at how detailed the instructions were. I knew in my belly that they must be carried out to the exact detail. I feared that if I didn't obey, the penalty would be great.

Let me explain. Is God some tyrant waiting for me to make one little mistake so He can clobber me over the head with a skillet or baseball bat? No, not at all. He gave me instructions to prepare me for the hardest trial of my life. It's been six years since I've lost my son. As soon as I became a watchman, there was a domino effect. The instructions were given to me in November 2012. A month and a half later, my youngest child took his life. That same week, a friend of mine who was like a father to me got very ill and needed care. Then the company where I worked for twenty-seven years announced they were closing. Had I not prayed for seven months the way He instructed, I never would have made it through. In my early walk with Jesus, I made numerous mistakes. God would give me simple instructions, for example, "Go tell this person you love them." I would procrastinate so long until the urge to do it left me, and I would deceive myself into believing that somehow God forgot He told me. Weeks later, I would hear on the news or from a friend that the person I was instructed to get in touch with died in some unforeseen tragedy. What followed that was guilt and shame that I could have intervened but didn't. After making about a half dozen more rebellious mistakes and seeing the horrific outcomes of my stubbornness, I was left feeling broken and defeated. I began to take a closer look at myself and saw how selfish I was, and I made a decision to listen when God speaks and obey.

Peace and Confidence

There is nothing more reassuring than knowing you did something right. With that comes an inner peace that allows you to relax and reap the benefits of making good choices. It has been six years since God gave me the instructions to pray for seven months. And it's because of the obedience of the people who chose to do the work and make the sacrifice and pay the price that the prayer line was birthed, and it's been a real blessing. After my assignment ended, my best friend, Willetta, felt led to carry it on all these years later because of the faithfulness of her and the others she prays with. I call them "The Chosen Prayer Warriors" (TCPW for short), aka "The Prayer Hogs." I don't know about you, but just knowing that someone is praying for me brings me peace. There are times that life can be very difficult, and you may feel as if you are about to have a breakdown. This message goes out especially to those of you who have already tried to take your life and to those who are contemplating the idea. We (TCPW) want you to know that you are important to us and we are praying for you, so take this peace and confidence that God wants for you and remember you are never alone. At the end of this book, you will find information about how to get support in your time of need.

Chapter 6

To the Suicide Survivor or Contemplator

The Last Straw

If you've ever heard someone say, "That's the last straw," when they've had enough or can't put up with something anymore, there's a back story to that expression, and it's about a camel. This working camel was weighted down with a heavy load on his back, and it was a very big burden for him. In fact, the weight was so heavy, and he carried it for so long, that he became very weary. And although he maintained such a heavy load for a good amount of time, his weariness finally got the best of him when someone (who didn't care to notice how tired he was) added one single extra straw to the pile on his back. That one straw made the weight of the entire burden too much for the camel, and he fell and broke his back. It's a good lesson for humans because we sometimes get trapped into doing what others expect or want from us. We carry out the tasks for different reasons and don't speak out against the heavy burdens put upon us. But our mouths have a purpose: to speak the truth, and we should. What heavy load or burden are you carrying right now that is about to break your back?

Being Honest

Sometimes people have a problem with transparency. We become so dependent upon other people for approval that we are afraid to say no for the sake of losing a friend. But would a true friend want you to be unhappy over a decision you aren't comfortable with? Not being honest can cause you much pain, just like it did the camel. You may be suffering in silence until one day your emotions break down, your strength is depleted, and there is nothing left but a shell of a person who just wants peace and rest. And you might have felt the quickest way to get relief was through self-destruction. I'm speaking to those who have attempted suicide before and failed. I'm sure the pain you were in was excruciating, but when your attempts were unsuccessful, you took a step back and had to face the fact that you are still here and wondered why. You tried so hard to escape the pain. Consider yourself very special and fortunate to still be breathing because now you have a story to share with others who may feel the same way.

Facing the Fear

You have made it past the step of ending it all, but what's next? Time to heal. It's a bold step, but you've already been in the darkest parts of your suffering. You tried to take your precious, God-given life. Now you must wake up, take a deep breath, stand up tall, and face the life you need to live. Take back your life gradually; begin by setting new boundaries that will protect you and your relationships.

Learning how to be honest about your feelings and how to effectively communicate with others will enhance your perception, and you will begin to grow in confidence and value your self-worth.

The Big Lie

"Nobody cares if I live or die," "I'm worthless," "I'll show them," "You're better off without me." These emotional thoughts and feelings are not true. Have you ever thought what the world would be like without you being here? You may think that your friends and loved ones would be better off without you, but you're wrong! You are in a state of only seeing things from one perspective. Now is the time to look at your accomplishments and not your failures. You have done or are doing something that is making a difference in someone else's life. Reflect on that right now. It may not even be a family member; it could be a neighbor, a classmate, a social worker, a friend, or a customer. You have value, and there would be a great void without you. This is the reality you must face.

The old movie *It's a Wonderful Life* provides a good example of what one person's life means to others. It's a story about a boy who grows up with big dreams to travel and see the world but instead ends up inheriting the family business, which he wants nothing to do with. He's forced into the situation when his father passes away. He is the oldest brother and has to take on the responsibility, which ends his dreams of traveling. Without giving away the whole story, he reaches a point where he wishes he had never been born and tries to take his own life. It's a great reminder that our lives are not worthless and that others see value in or receive some sort of inspiration from our presence. If you are afraid of your future, you aren't alone. But your future is your next step in the right direction, so take it! Fear is your enemy only when you allow it to hold you back. It can be your friend when you put it behind you to give you a push. Without the resistance of fear, there is nothing to conquer. A friend of mine often told me, "Your car runs on a battery, and that battery has a negative side and a positive side. But it can't run without both." Life is a fight to the finish, and it is a challenge. But remember, you are never alone.

Disfigured and Scarred

"Whatcha See Is Whatcha Get" is a song that was popular in the seventies by The Dramatics. The lyrics mean that what you're looking at is real and not an imitation. I am not faking; I am who I say that I am. That's actually one of God's famous lines! You may be scarred, but so was Jesus. Wear your scar like a testimony. I don't mean you have to show it off to everyone you meet, but it is your testimony, your story, and you are a survivor. You made it, but that doesn't mean you don't have challenging days ahead; it just means you're still here and you beat the odds. You have purpose, and it's time to move forward. No matter how visible your scar is, it's now a part of your testimony, of what almost happened to you, and now you are alive to share with others who may be feeling hopeless. Sometimes you see photos of people proudly showing their scars; they may be cancer survivors, veterans of war, or survivors of some other difficult trauma. They display their scars as a way to show they are courageous overcomers who have embraced the changes they've been through. This helps them move forward. They can't change what's been done to them, but they can change how they handle their scars. Isaiah 61:3 (NLT) states, "To all who mourn in Israel, He will give a crown of beauty for ashes, a joyous blessing instead of mourning, festive praise instead of despair. In their righteousness, they will be like great oaks that the Lord has planted for His own glory."

Finding Support

Every single person on God's green earth has met some sort of challenge and has been in need of support. This is why there are so many support groups to choose from. Keep in mind that support groups are run by people and people are not perfect, so it's wise to visit several different ones to find out which one works best for you. When in pursuit of looking for the right support group or counselor, remember to take your time; patience is key. "Good things do eventually come to those who wait." Finding support is a part of the success package we all need for a successful life. By successful, I don't mean only material gain, such as fancy cars, big boats, or a large bank account. Real success is finding peace within yourself. If you give the Bible a chance, you'll find out it's a pretty amazing book. It has every problem in it; it's about people like you and me that have issues, and in spite of them, God still loves us all. Ecclesiastes 4:9-11 (ESV) tells us, "Two are better than one, because they have a good reward for their toil. For if one falls, one will lift up his fellow man. But woe to him who is alone when he falls and has not another to lift him up!" Galatians 6:2 (ESV) states, "Bear one another's burdens, and so fulfill the law of Christ." So, you see that support is vital for growth. God created us for relationships, not to be loners. Don't get me wrong. Being alone to gather your thoughts is great, but running from people and hiding your feelings is dangerous. I'm not suggesting you tell everyone your every thought, but it's important to share your negative or destructive thoughts and feelings and get support before they lead you down a dangerous path.

Chapter 7

Material Gain

Understanding Your Worth

Your life has no price tag because you are irreplaceable. The things we go into debt for only have price tags. We live in a world full of luxury items and interesting gadgets. We have cars with cameras to see what's coming, that can brake for us if necessary, and some that even park themselves. We have home security devices that allow us to see our homes in real time from anywhere in the world. Humans definitely love material things. So much so that we're willing to spend more time working so we can buy more toys to play with. We compare ourselves to others who have more than us and try to keep up with them or surpass them. This can cause extra stress in our lives because if we don't get the promotion or the better paying job, we feel like we aren't as good as the next person who is able to buy all the expensive luxuries. This is a tricky trap we allow ourselves to get into. It happens before we realize we've taken the bait, so beware of material desires that may cause you added stress.

You are the highest form of creation. Humans were given dominion over animals in Genesis 1:28, which states, "God blessed them [Adam and Eve] and said to them, 'Be fruitful and increase in number; fill the earth and subdue it. Rule over the fish in the sea and the birds in the sky and over every living creature that moves on the ground.'" Of course, God did not mean that we should ever be mean or abusive to animals at any time, but we are to use them in a respectful and appropriate manner.

Human organs are very valuable. All over the world you will find long lists of people who are in need of new organs because the ones they were born with have malfunctioned somehow from wear and tear or faulty genetics and they are in need of a functional body part. Organ transplant operations are pricey, not just in dollars and cents, but because your life has no price tag and no amount of money can equal the true worth of your life. I researched the prices of organs, and discovered that not only is the organ itself expensive, but that the procedure can range from hundreds of thousands of dollars into the millions. So to even ponder the thought of feeling worthless is ridiculous. You are the highest valued form of existence on earth. Never think lowly of yourself again because if God made you in His likeness, you're crafted by the best.

Stay determined to get through your pain. The season you are in is like the weather—it will change. When fall comes, we know winter is just around the corner. When winter is here, we know springtime is next, and then summer. Change is a part of life, and the lessons we learn from those changes help us grow. The pain you are feeling right now is just a season and will change. Fight through your pain and don't give up. Learn to trust God with your fragmented heart.

Chapter 8

Organ Donor Recipients and Their Stories

I'm sure you've heard the old saying that there are two things you can count on in this life: death and taxes. Though both are surely to come, lowering your taxes is something we all can accomplish in time, and death should only come to us when it is our true appointed time. Please get the help that you need to not end your life on your own terms (the role of God has already been taken). Stay determined to get through your pain. Once again, the season you are in is a lot like the weather—it will surely change. How you are feeling right now will pass. It's impossible for things to remain exactly the same. Change is a part of life, and the lessons we learn from those changes help us grow. Learn to trust God with your fragmented heart. In my research, I've found there are over 100,000 people on organ-donor waiting lists hoping for a better quality of life and holding on to the dream of continuing life's journey to complete their God-given assignment (and we all have one; whether we realize it or not).

Over the past three decades, I have met several people who either needed an organ transplant or were organ donors. Three of those people are coworkers or friends I have known for a number of years. My friend and coworker Toni had been having trouble with her eyes for over ten years. Our job required a lot of finding people and places and writing down instructions. She struggled with trying to keep up with all the demands of the occupation as long as she could, but when driving later became an unpleasant task, she finally had to take an early retirement option. After consulting with several surgeons, she decided to get a cornea transplant, and the results were amazing. She was once again able to drive and handle her personal responsibilities independently. Unfortunately, the results were short-lived, and she has had to have four additional surgeries to keep her eyesight. She is now eighty-four years old, and her first operation was over twenty years ago.

I had another coworker whose twelve-year-old niece became suddenly ill while at school and had to be airlifted by helicopter to the hospital for emergency surgery. She had a successful kidney transplant procedure but had to limit her activity and watch her diet.

My dear friend Susie's son, Donell, is like a brother to me. We used to hang out together when we were younger. One day while he was waiting for me at a venue, he saw an attractive lady behind a registration desk and thought he would try to see if she would give him her phone number. After the smooth talker laid out his charm, she pulled out a pen and paper and wrote it down for him. Donell, my friend, was a hard one to catch, but she had what it took; nearly thirty years later, they are still together. In the early years of their marriage, Donell became chronically ill; his kidneys were failing, and he needed an organ donor. The love between him and his wife was so strong that she wanted to help, so she went to get tested to see if she was a match and found out she was in fact the perfect candidate for her husband. The two of them talked among themselves then spoke with family, and the decision was made to give the surgery a go at the Mayo Clinic; the outcome was successful. The procedure was done successfully, and they literally have a piece of one another. This makes the scripture Mark 10:8 really come alive!

And the two will become one flesh, so they are no longer two but one flesh.
(Mark 10:8)

My best friend, Willetta, has a cousin named Iva. Iva and her brother Peerless were always very close. As the years progressed, Peerless needed a kidney transplant, and his sister was able to give him one of her kidneys. She told Willetta and me the story of how her brother got sick and how her kidney was able to save him. She said, "I would do it all again just to have him near me," and in that moment, I thought, *Wow, that is a true love commitment.*

Greater love has no one than this; to lay down one's life for one's friends. (John 15:13)

The last two stories about Donell and his wife and Willetta's cousins really showcase what true love and commitment are all about. It reminds me of an old funny story (on the light side of things). This story is about a pig and a chicken. One day, the two got into a big argument on this farm about breakfast, and they went back and forth arguing who was the most committed to the meal. After going back and forth for a number of minutes, the pig got really stirred up, leaned over to the chicken coop from his muddy pen, slid his hoof inside the wire of the fence, and said, "All you do is lay eggs all day long for breakfast! As soon as you lay 'em, they come from the farmhouse to get 'em! Then you cluck around your coop then go back and lay some more. But when they come from the farmhouse to get me, it's ham or bacon...I'm cooked!" You've gotta admit, the pig's all in, and those that are still living that donate and share organs to help others are real heroes. What a gift of love.

The last transplant story is about my dear friend Veronica. We worked together for several years and became close friends. She was and still is very conscientious about her appearance and well-being. She was always joyous and a pleasure to be around and didn't have any health restrictions that I knew of. One day, in her Bahamian accent (she is from Freeport, Grand Bahamas), she called my name from across the room to feel her hands because she was experiencing a great deal of discomfort. She knew I was a part-time reflexologist and could use pressure point therapy for circulation issues. I had helped her with this in the past, so she was confident I could assist this time. I took both of her hands in mine and was surprised to find her skin felt cold, stiff, and lifeless. She looked at me expectantly, believing that one of my brief massages would be the solution to her issue. And although the massage did bring her some temporary relief, she later ended up in the hospital having numerous tests. After two or three weeks of ending up in the hospital when her symptoms became unmanageable, a specialist was contacted, and he diagnosed her with a rare autoimmune condition in which the body produces too much collagen, causing the skin and connective tissue to thicken. There is no natural cure for this horrible disorder (scleroderma). It began to take over her body to the point of her flat lining, but a faithful family friend who was by her bedside insisted that the emergency team try resuscitating her one final time. This act of persistence is why she is alive today! The disease caused her to be in desperate need of a kidney, and she was on a waiting list for several years. She waited patiently and took extra care of her health. Then the phone call came that a kidney was available, and interestingly enough, the call came on the same day my son's organs were extracted and flown to somewhere in Washington state. We don't believe she has his kidney because we were told his organs would stay within the state and she lives in Florida, but what a special bond we share of giving and receiving the enrichment of life on the very same day.

Veronica continues to live a courageous life. She has written two books so far, one on the importance of nutrition titled *My Daily Life, Back to Life*. It's a wonderful book full of recipes that are rich in nutrients and alkaline-based foods. These recipes have helped aid her in her quest to a healthier life, and they are also very tasty! This diet is how she maintains her health, since there is no cure. Her second book has not yet been published but is about how she died and came back to life. If you are interested in learning more about Veronica's road to recovery, she can be reached at ronnie.87@hotmail.com or https://yhealthysnacks41ife.com.

Showing Gratitude for a Second Chance

I've witnessed the struggles and hardships of my coworkers and friends and their families and how they strive every day to live. They've made sacrifices because they want to live. They've stopped smoking, drinking, and eating unhealthy foods, or at least eating a very minimum of those. My friend Toni protects her eyes with special glasses and is on a well-balanced diet. Willetta's cousin has become almost exclusively vegan, except for sometimes eating a small amount of meat. She is in her seventies and looks and feels great. Donell has improved his diet as well. Veronica has made healthy eating a way of life and helps to educate others. These people almost nearly didn't make it, but they are fighting to stay here. That's what I would love to see you do. Get the help you need and change your lifestyle so you can learn how to enjoy this God-given gift of life. These people have learned to focus on the most important things in life, and those aren't material things or possessions. Rather, the most important things in life are your inner actions and your relationship with the Creator. If things are right with Him, He can guide you through life, and you will have peace and joy; the right relationships will come in time as you grow, or you will begin to grow the relationships you already have into better relationships.

Cell Memory Fact or Fiction

If you believe in the miracle of creation like I do, you will be familiar with the Bible teachings in the book of Genesis that God created the heaven and the earth and mankind. Our bodies have amazing abilities. Even if you believe only in science, you know and understand that the body is made up of trillions of cells, among other amazing things, to hold it together. Cells are the basic building blocks to all living things. They provide structure for our bodies and take nutrients from food to convert them into energy. Dr. Andrew Armor, a heart specialist, noticed that there is a presence of neurons in the heart. Neurons are electrically excitable cells that send more information to other parts of the body. Most importantly, he discovered that the heart actually sends more information to the brain than the other way around. You can find more information about this in Dr. Armor's book, *Neurocardiology: Anatomical and Functional Principles.*[4] I know this information may shock some of you because you may think the brain is the only means we have of creating thought, but if you look up scriptures, you will find verses like this: "O generation of vipers, how can ye being evil, speak good things? For out of the abundance of the heart the mouth speaketh" (Matt. 12:34, KJV). You may be thinking that your brain does all the thinking and not your heart. But Jeremiah 17:9-10 (NIV) tells us our hearts and minds are connected.

Dr. Paul Pearsall researched the cell memory theory and discovered that organ donor recipients receive much more than just an organ. He found that they also receive what he calls "cellular memories." These types of memories have had extraordinary manifestations in organ transplant recipients. Even if you are a skeptic, it's hard to argue with an actual cellular memory experience. My friend Veronica, for instance, starting having repeated dreams about a little boy shortly after having the organ transplant operation. She also began having unusual cravings for dainties, even though she has never been a big eater of sweet foods. She later discovered that the kidney she received was from a little boy who liked sweets very much.

Donell was never a big talker, but one day he was going on and on about all sorts of different things, and the person he was talking to seemed irritated. He didn't understand why, but his wife said, "Honey, to be honest, ever since you got my kidney, you've been very chatty." That's when he realized that there is really something to this cell memory experience.

There are many testimonials about people seeing their donors in dreams. In fact, Chloe, who received my son's lung, said she had a message from my son that she needed to deliver to me. She explained that she sought me out so persistently because she felt as if she would burst if she didn't give me this message from Reese that he profoundly loved me. And believe me, it came at a time when I really needed reassuring.

Meeting Chloe, My Son's Lung Recipient

Andre Crouch is a famous gospel artist I used to listen to often while growing up. He wrote a song called "Thank You Lord." The song is based on the following scripture:

One day, Jesus was traveling along the border between Samaria and Galilee on the way to Jerusalem. As he was going into a village, ten lepers met him. They stood at a distance and shouted, "Jesus, Master, have mercy on us!"

When Jesus saw them, he told them, "Go and show yourselves to the priests." While they were going, they were made clean. But one of them, when he saw that he had been healed, came back and praised God with a loud voice. He fell on his face at Jesus' feet and thanked him. Now that man was a Samaritan.

Jesus asked, "Ten men were made clean, weren't they? Where are the other nine? Except for this foreigner, were any of them found to return and give praise to God? Then he told the man, "Get up, and go home! Your faith has saved you."   (Luke 17:11-19, ISV)

This is a very interesting story for several reasons. Samaritans and Jews didn't get along, but yet Jesus healed him and he reached out to be healed. When you think about it, differences shouldn't matter when there is a real need.

The particular part of this story I would like to highlight is about the leper who voiced his gratitude. The scripture lets us know there were nine others with him, but yet only he returned. When my son's organs were brought to Washington state, our family was told his organs would probably save around a hundred lives. That's a lot of people! But yet out of all of those people, only one pursued me to thank our family for his generous donation. I do believe he was in soundness of mind when he made the decision to be a donor because he had a deep compassion for others. Let me explain that I understand that chasing down your donor's family can be a bit risky and unpredictable. I am just giving an example of heartfelt gratitude. Chloe really wanted a life extension to complete her assignment here on earth, and her prayers were answered. She pursued me with such passion until I gave in to wanting to contact her back. She showed such tenacious grace and was careful and kind with respect for my feelings and my privacy, and for that I am very grateful because if she hadn't reached out to me, I never would have gotten a chance to meet such a well-deserving friend. I admit, in the beginning, the idea of meeting her was totally out of the question. Just the idea of my son's lung inside someone else's chest was enough to make me faint at the very thought of such a thing. But the day finally came. We both were very nervous, but we gave each other such a gripping hug. Her lung (Reese's) breathed in and out fast and strong. After our hugs, we had a delicious meal, and we became family because now we share some of the same DNA.

The New Normal

After the emotional shock of losing your loved one and the funeral or memorial service is completed, you have a lot to deal with. Your life has been altered, and you have to search to find a brand new normal. Some of the things you will find yourself doing are looking at your phone to see if your deceased loved one has called you or walking into a store and seeing someone who looks like your loved one, and your heart begins to race. When this happens, you might feel as though you are in a dream or daze. These things are normal, and you will have to learn to process your experiences in a healthy way so they don't control you. You must focus on the positive things in life. If you lost a child like I did, then I suggest you focus on your living children. Try to become closer to them and bring them nearer to you if they will allow you to, because they too are processing their own pain. Everyone deals with loss differently, so it's important to respect their boundaries as you work on your own healing. We all heal at different speeds and levels. Some people may expect you to be over certain feelings right away and may become impatient with you. Don't get bothered by that. Some people lack deep compassion and understanding, and some are just not good at dealing with things of this magnitude. That doesn't mean they don't care about you. They may just process their pain a little differently. Also, remember, you are vulnerable right now, so please be careful not to make any big decisions right away. You are too emotional for that. And don't let anyone pressure you. Take a step back until you feel more stable.

Chapter 9

The Misunderstood Motives of Others

People who are grieving with you can react to your loss of your friend, partner, or family member in seemingly strange ways. Say, for instance, a coworker or family member asks you what you are going to do with your lost loved one's clothes and belongings. You may still be in shock or pain, and this question may seem very insensitive. But you should consider that this person has had a loss as well, and they share the same feelings of wanting to have this person near them again, just like you do. Owning the home they once lived in or possessing, wearing, or owning the clothes, jewelry, car, etc. helps aid them in their healing process as well. It's not always that people who ask you these things are prowling piranhas! Try to practice giving the request some thought. That way, if it comes up again in conversation, you can be prepared to handle it well, because your loved one had life experiences with other people besides you. When we are hurting, we can sometimes shut other people out and inflict unnecessary pain on them without even trying. It's important to consider other people's pain when a family member passes away. A lot of their belongings were shared by others who loved and valued them. You can pick and choose what to give them, but try to be as understanding as you can, because everyone is at the height of their emotions during this time.

(left to right): Willetta, Reese's godmother; Genesis; and Gabrielle, a.k.a G'Bell

"Genesis and Reese".

"Genesis, Reese's older brother".

"Reese's promo card".

"G'Bell singing at Jesus Is the Answer Ministries in Las Vegas, with Reese playing the drums and Ramon on keyboard".

"Reese on drums at Jesus Is the Answer Ministries as a young teen".

"Reese AKA Frijiea at one of his shows on stage".

"On stage at another show".

"Another show on stage".

"Clowning around at a grocery store with one of his clients as a caregiver".

"Reese's uncle Glen, far left; me, his mother, Gabrielle; and Reese, far right; with a restaurant owner in Little Rock, Arkansas".

"Reese and me at my graduation from Travel & Tourism, 1996".

"Reese and Genesis performing together in Spokane, Washington".

"Reese, far right, performing with other artists in Spokane".

"Reese and me after church at Jesus Is the Answer Ministries hanging out with the youth".

'Picture of Reese as Frijiea (middle, sitting) with former professional group "Truce".

"Another picture of Frijiea (far left) with Truce".

Chapter 10

Maurice, AKA Reese (Baby Boy)

Reese's Passion Pets

Some people are so magnetic that when they enter a room, they grab the attention of others almost immediately. You see this quality often in leaders. There is just something about these people that give out light to others. If that sounds like you or someone you know, then you just met Maurice, aka Reese, my youngest son. Both of my sons have this personality type. Reese always had great compassion for others. He loved animals and was the child who would try to fix the broken wing of a bird and would consistently try to talk me into taking in a stray dog or cat. One day when he was much younger, we were walking with some friends and family members on a sidewalk near a church, and we suddenly heard a strange sound behind us. We looked back, and about fifty yards away, we saw a white furry creature running swiftly toward us. We all scattered in multiple directions. I must admit that I'm not so brave to show compassion to an animal that is chasing me, especially one that I can't even identify. I had never seen a four-legged creature of this sort, and because it was running in our direction, keeping myself and my children from harm's way was all that I could think about. I screamed as loud as I could, "Capture the beast!" And someone yelled back, "I got this." I don't recall who it was, but some quick-thinking and brave hero picked up an empty garbage can and trapped the mysterious beast inside it.

I finally caught my breath, and my racing heart began to go back to its normal rhythm patterns. I asked what on earth the creature was, and someone said it sort of resembled a fox. Someone else thought it was a long white squirrel. And the next thing I heard was, "Mom, can we keep it?" I couldn't believe that little Reese would ask such a thing when most of us had just had the scare of the decade. In disbelief and shock, the words from my trembling lips uttered, "Keep it? We don't even know what it is." But you know how the irresistible sweetness of a child who grabs your shirttail or pant leg just the right way, with just the right angle of sunlight beaming down upon your child's head, can sway you. You look down into your child's round, chubby face and into his eyes so round and bright and innocent, and the war begins inside you. The word no is on the tip of your tongue, but it won't press through because now you're staring into those big brown eyes and you can hear the angels singing, and the battle inside you intensifies. At first, the word yes begins to slip through your lips, but then you realize that would be absurd, then the no rolls forward and it's a mind-and-tongue war. You're asking yourself, "Why you don't just say no?" But you can't because your heart feels like it's growing bigger and bigger in just seconds. So a big yes rolls right off my tongue, just like a bowling ball headed for a strike down the alley.

The shock and feelings of dread were upon me, but it was too late because the commitment had been made. All of a sudden, the sunlight was gone, the music stopped, and terror was in control because I had no clue what I had just said yes to. My brave child flipped the garbage can over, and I was frightened he may get bitten and get rabies; but none of that mattered to him. He scooped up this strange-looking creature, held it close, and stroked its fur, and the rest was history. He had himself a new fuzzy friend. He was beaming from ear to ear, and I looked like I swallowed a log. I was so mad at myself for saying yes to something that wasn't planned and so abrupt, and I wondered how on earth I was going to feel safe and comfortable in the same house with this four-legged creature I had never seen before. I knew that rules that I could live with had to be implemented. Rule number one was we had to get a pet cage and find out just what kind of animal this was. After several days of this new guest living in our home, we noticed an awful odor coming from him, so I did what any young mother would do when something or someone smelled: I gave it a bath and sprayed it with perfume! What an experience! That animal's body would shrink then get long again. It was giving me goosebumps. I had never seen anything like this before, but after some research, we discovered we had a ferret (a domesticated skunk), so it's no wonder he smelled bad! It didn't take long for me to talk my son out of keeping his new pet. We made a few calls and found a new home for my son's short-lived fluffy ferret friend.

While on the subject of his love for pets, Reese's last three beloved animals were his light-brown Chihuahua named Coco, who was very temperamental; his very stout, muscular, light-tan pit bull named Carlito, who was playful, energetic, and smart (Reese always pronounced Carlito's name with a Mexican accent that was so adorable); and his exotic lizard that resembled a miniature dinosaur and somehow got out of his cage from time to time. I had warned my son that his lizard had better not get out of that cage when I came to visit and stay the night. Besides his grand admiration for all the animals of the world, Reese had many other interests and talents.

The Donor Saves Lives and Shows Compassion

Reese's father had a love for motorcycles, and he bought a brand new Honda when Reese was young. It was a bright, shiny red color, and Reese would sit on it and pretend he was driving it. One day, while no one was paying close attention, he figured he would take it out for a spin. He couldn't have been more than three or four, which meant he wasn't even tall enough to reach the pedals, but being the adventurous type, he didn't let that stop him. Somehow, he managed to get it started

63

but lost control of it and headed straight for the garage door. One crash and boom later, that was the end of the bike. Thank God he wasn't hurt.

Years later, he hadn't lost his love and attraction for motorcycles. He bought a green and black Kawasaki and drove it like a ninja. He joined a motorcycle club named Rough Riders. Some of his Rough Rider buddies were at my son's memorial service and honored him with a leather Rough Rider jacket that I'm sure he would have worn with great admiration had he been there to receive it. He also loved to swim. He was also a trophy-winning pool player. He had a pool table inside his recording studio. He loved to play basketball and would encourage and mentor young kids on how to become a more valuable player. Reese was no angel—he had many faults like the rest of us—but he appeared to love life and people. With all his zest for life, we were left puzzled as to how he could leave us this way. These are the mysteries and the dark side of our loved ones. They love and enjoy life then get stuck in a place of no return. They appear to value their own life less than others' lives and put animals and other people and things above themselves.

Here is an example of how valuable he felt others were. While I was visiting Reese one afternoon, he shared a story of how he took a young man with him to a show he was performing in, and after his performance, he asked the young man if he wanted to catch a ride back or if he would like to hang out for the after party. The young man chose to stay and hang out. My son said he was tired because it had been a very long week and he just wanted to go home and rest, so he waved goodbye to the young man and gave handshakes and hugs to others and proceeded toward the elevator. Seconds after the elevator door shut, he heard gunshots and people screaming. The elevator door then opened, and he saw people running to get inside in a panic. He saw another young man lying in a puddle of blood (not the young man he had brought to the show) and surrounded by several people pulling his arm and slapping his face for him to wake up. He ran toward the man yelling for people to move aside because he was a trained medical technician. He got down on the floor and began CPR, and he said when the young man began to breathe, a long stream of blood squirted into the air and he opened his eyes. He began to speak, and the young man's girlfriend began to weep and thank my son. An ambulance arrived and took the man. People thanked and hugged him for what he did. He asked for this young man's mother's phone number so he could check on his progress. An hour or so later, he called and left a message and got a call back shortly afterward from the young man's mother telling him it didn't end the way they had hoped, and she thanked him for all his efforts to save her son's life. She told him that although he lost the fight to stay here with his family and friends, he at least he got a chance to see his loved ones one last time before he entered eternity.

My son's girlfriend told me about another thing Reese had done just days before he decided to end his life. He noticed a man face down in the snow on a sidewalk, and as he got closer, he noticed lots of blood coming from this man's head. Apparently, he had been struck from behind, possibly robbed and left for dead. Reese pulled off his own jacket and applied the correct amount of pressure to the head wound, resuscitated the man, and waited with him until the ambulance arrived. I have committed the stories that friends and family have shared of his heroic rescues and acts of generosity to memory. Reese's day job was as a healthcare provider, and from what I'm told, he was passionate about providing the best of care to his patients. One of my favorite stories about my son was that he threw away all of the old worn-out shoes of all of his patients. There is this thing in our family about old worn-out shoes. We just don't like them. It is a tradition in my family to buy plenty of shoes because it shows you are particular about your appearance. As the story goes, the patients were looking for their grungy shoes and were about ready to go into an uproar when Reese made the announcement he had a present for everyone and to meet him in the multipurpose room. The patients made their way to the room, and Reese presented each one with a shoebox containing a brand-new pair of shoes, bought to match each patient's taste. They cheered and clapped, and a bonding took place that my son and the patients appreciated for years to come. But even during these times, I wonder if he was fighting negative thoughts and if he really knew how important his life was to everyone else who knew him, as well as how much people loved him and enjoyed his company.

Accepting the Unacceptable: A Change of Focus

On day four at the hospital, I had to accept that my son would never breathe another voluntary breath, sing another song, dribble another basketball, dance to another beat, befriend another animal, or face another challenge in this world. My sister and I had prayed all night long for a miracle, but when the sun rose up over the hills and shone through the evergreen trees the next morning and there were still no signs of voluntary movement coming from the hospital bed where my baby boy was lying, I had to face the reality and rely on God's strength in my weakness. As my sister and I looked each other in the eyes, she put her right hand over her heart in a gesture of how hurt and disappointed she was and how broken she knew I was. I mimicked the gesture, and we both stood up at the same time and changed our postures to that of a firm, soldier-type erectness, as if to say to those who may have thought we wouldn't survive the discouraging outcome that we were strong in God. I wrote this poem after that experience.

Spiritual Soldier

I'm in a fight each and every day
sometimes it's hard to see my way
but since I'm a soldier
I can't give up the fight
I must march right through it
Whether day or night

even when it's foggy and I can't see my way
even if the sunlight blinds me with its brilliant ray

through the noise through the rocks
and through the mud
through the sweat and tears
and spilt blood

Sometimes through the fire
up and down a mountain slope
in a ditch through barbed wire
I cling tightly to endless hope.
I remind myself soon the war will end
and my joy will be restored
and I'll find peace again
but right now I'm on the battlefield
with sword and shield I stand
and I must keep on fighting
until the victory at last I win.

In this life there are wars to fight
some seem fair
some not right
but in this warlike life
we fight for success
and we win some
we lose some
and it all causes stress.

But because I'm a soldier
I can never just stop
'cause I'm protecting something bigger
than the urge to let things drop

Someone will be needing the protection I provide
then others will run for cover, and some will bleed and die.

This is the role I've been given in the army of the Lord
to fight these supernatural battles with weapons like my sword

The B.I.B.L.E.
That's the sword for me
it keeps me from my own methods
that lead back to adolescence
to stay grounded
assured and matured
it reminds me that I'm Godly
still standing strong yet pure

Thank God death isn't final
Jesus conquered the grave!
He's the resurrected soldier
who made rude death behave

So I'll stand here on my post
until eternity calls
and salute my General Father
because He always stays involved

Then in time step forward
when the General calls my name
to pin me with purple honors
for all my agonizing pain

and just like a soldier
I'll stand up straight and tall
to rejoice in all my battles
because right then it'll be worth it all!

And just like soldiers, we grabbed the hands of my son and kissed him once again on his chubby cheeks. By this time, the surgical team had entered the room and had witnessed our solemn surrender to at last do what they came to do. The nursing team nodded for our approval to prepare to wheel him away. One of the nurses came over to my side to comfort me. I once again gave the cue it was time to say goodbye, and this set it all in motion. We all slowly left the room then one nurse released the wheel brakes on the bed as another carefully unplugged and rearranged certain devices, and very slowly and casually, they left the room we had grown accustomed to for our three-night and four-day stay and went down the hall and around the corner.

My eyes watched every motion made. The handsome doctor was the first to reach the elevator. He paused then firmly pushed the button, and the arrow lit up. Then he turned to me and said, "We are going to take very good care of him. He'll be riding in style tonight on a private plane." I smiled as the tears began to fill my eyes and said, "He'll really enjoy that. He always loved to travel first class." Then the elevator door opened, and I stood watching as the medical team carefully positioned the hospital bed snugly inside before they shut the door. The surgeon looked up at me once again and said, "We will take good care of him. Today his heart will be flown to a town hundreds of miles away within the state of Washington to save a life early in the morning, and the total amount of lives that will be saved because of his excellent health will be over one hundred." I nodded my head gently as I continued to watch through my tears as the door shut. It was only a matter of minutes, but it felt like a marathon goodbye. I think I stood there watching the elevator until the light disappeared then I turned and faced my sister. Our eyes met, we locked arms, and we turned and walked away with a strange type of soothing satisfaction that you get when you have done your best but the outcome wasn't what you wanted.

After leaving the hospital, I felt such a sense of loss and heaviness. While getting ready for bed, I tried to envision my son alive and breathing, and while I was trying to imagine this, I had a vision of the sky lit up with tiny twinkling stars. It made me think of Abraham and God's promise to him when He spoke to Abraham to look up and behold the stars. Genesis 26:4-5 states, "I will make your descendants as numerous as the stars in the sky and will give them all these lands, and through your offspring all nations on earth will be blessed, because Abraham obeyed me and did everything I required of him, keeping my commands and my decrees and my instructions." Of course, this was a situation of completely different circumstances, but it showed me how God still kept His promise to me by saving my son in his final hours and how he helped numerous people even under these devastating circumstances. While looking upward, I heard the Lord tell me that even though my son was with Him in heaven, his actual body never really experienced death because his live organs went inside others' struggling bodies, and those parts of him are alive.

I never would have thought of this. He is still here and in more places than he ever has been before. Then another thought came to mind. We are created in God's image and in His likeness, and we are part of Him, so that means God isn't just everywhere but He lives and breathes in us as well.

It hit me that my son's lungs, heart, kidneys, skin, eyes, etc. were alive but in someone else. I had never experienced anyone in my family being an organ donor besides my son. It was a mind-blowing experience for me to realize that my son's organs were responsible for giving life! I will never look at organ donations the same again.

Chapter 11

Piecing It All Together

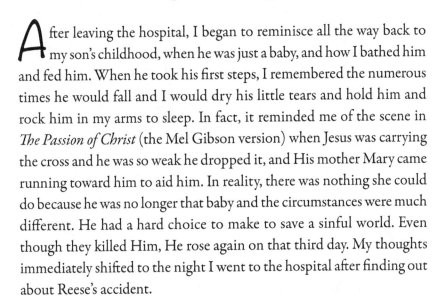

After leaving the hospital, I began to reminisce all the way back to my son's childhood, when he was just a baby, and how I bathed him and fed him. When he took his first steps, I remembered the numerous times he would fall and I would dry his little tears and hold him and rock him in my arms to sleep. In fact, it reminded me of the scene in *The Passion of Christ* (the Mel Gibson version) when Jesus was carrying the cross and he was so weak he dropped it, and His mother Mary came running toward him to aid him. In reality, there was nothing she could do because he was no longer that baby and the circumstances were much different. He had a hard choice to make to save a sinful world. Even though they killed Him, He rose again on that third day. My thoughts immediately shifted to the night I went to the hospital after finding out about Reese's accident.

While Genesis's friend drove me to the hospital, his friend shared a story about how his sister had passed away just a few years prior and expressed that he understood our pain and was there to do whatever he could to help ease the pain we were experiencing. I told him my only focus was getting my son up out of that bed and off the ventilator machine and hearing him call me "Mama" once again. I told him I needed some blessed anointing oil as found in the scriptures (from the ESV versions) Mark 6:13 and James 5:14: "'Is anyone among you sick? Let him call for the elders of the church, and let them pray over

71

him, anointing him with oil in the name of the Lord.' And they cast out many demons and anointed with oil many who were sick and healed them." I strongly believe in this because it's in the Bible, of course, but because I happen to know two people that flatlined and are alive and going on in life with their second chance now, grateful and living it to the fullest. Yes, miracles do happen, and this was my witness. What this young man offered me was so heartfelt and sincere. He said he would call his godfather who is a minister to see if he could help. The young man hit speed dial on his phone, put his godfather on speaker, asked him for the oil, and in just a matter of minutes, my request for blessed anointing oil was answered. What is blessed anointing oil? It is simply oil that has been prayed over by godly people. Authentic anointing oil has a recipe, and it's found in Exodus (30:23-24). I'm not sharing this to say that if this particular recipe isn't followed, it's not truly blessed oil, because with the prayer of faith, you could probably use Crisco and get the same results. I'm sharing to inform you this is how they did it in the Bible. Some people use plain olive oil, some make their own, and some buy it, like the minister who gave me his bottle.

Soothing Supernatural Comfort

After the dust began to settle, I continued to search for answers. My mind traveled back to the scene of the hospital on that vulnerable evening of the tragedy. On arrival, I was guided quickly to the ICU floor. My son Reese, also known by his stage name, Frijiea, being a somewhat renowned musician, had a following. There were a sea of fans and friends standing throughout the hallways. Some loved him, and some loved his music; they both were there to show their love and support. The hospital staff was excellent, which made it so much easier to weather the storm we were all in. The staff could see they had someone that was loved and cared for because of the enormous crowd. The staff showed so much patience and generosity. They could see that this young man had touched many lives. People were standing in the hallways awaiting a good report in spite of his split decision to end his life. On day four, myself and others prayed the prayer of faith that he would be resurrected just like Christ or Lazarus when Jesus called him to come forth from the tomb on the third day. But on that fourth morning (I gave it an extra day), when his body was lying there still and the only movement was the ventilator machine forcing his motionless body up and down with the artificial air in his lungs, I was ready to accept that I had done all that I could do. I experienced the love and support of family and friends that rallied around us like a shield. It was one of the most opportune times one could show true love and support, and it was heartfelt and appreciated.

While spending most of my time at the hospital during those four days, I got familiar with the faces (I'm not good with names) of nurses. This one lady was hanging around quite a bit while our family and friends had discussions in the family room area. My focus was my son, so I didn't think to ask certain questions about who was who right away. However, when I began to ask those types of questions, I discovered there were people there from the organ donor place (Northwest Life Center) and that the lady sitting inside the family room with us most of the time was a counselor. She stayed in the background and observed our behaviors.

Trying to keep all the supernatural occurrences to one chapter has been a challenge all through writing this book because just about everything we went through was divine. Yet, another one happened while we were all sitting in the family room. The counselor began to recall to us stories she had witnessed of passed-on loved ones who left some sort of signs that they were near, watching and listening. The stories she shared were inspirational, but I really wasn't expecting anything like that, at least not so soon anyway.

To my right, there was a rather large aquarium that was built into the wall. Genesis, my best friend, and Reese's girlfriend were facing me with the fish tank between us. It couldn't have been more than ten or twenty seconds after the counselor said to look for a sign Reese was near us that something strange and unusual happened. There were several fish in this tank but only two that resembled golden angelfish. All of a sudden, one of the fish began to break-dance inside this tank! It sounds crazy, I know. My son was in gymnastics in his early years and loved to dance, so he always incorporated flips, splits, and cartwheels, etc. in his dance routines. Now I had never seen a fish break-dance, and I never even knew it was possible. So, when I saw this fish move like he was flipping and turning cartwheels then moonwalk across the fish tank in a straight stride, I couldn't believe what I was witnessing. I jumped out of my chair and yelled, "Did anyone see that?" I think only one person did, I don't remember who, but I told everyone to come stand around the tank because I knew I wasn't cuckoo! So everyone rushed over and assembled around the tank with high anticipation he would do it again. We all set our eyes on that angelfish and waited for him to give us his fishtail version of some of my son's favorite dance moves. And wouldn't you know, just seconds later, he began to swarm the waters with his flips and fancy floating back strokes, and then, of course, for his grand finale, he did the moonwalk. We all were roaring around that tank like we were at a Grammy Awards celebration because not one of us had ever witnessed such a sight in our entire lives. That put the icing on the cake that night; it lifted our spirits to new heights that God would let us witness His marvelous signs and wonders to put our minds at ease. I don't believe in ghosts lingering around in hallways; in fact, I believe that's probably demonic. But God has a way of allowing things such as this to bring us comfort, joy, and peace, and that is what we all experienced that evening.

Chapter 12

The Loss of a Loved One

W e all have a limited amount of time on earth, and we all must go when it is our appointed time. Those people that are left behind have to bear the responsibility of making the arrangements to ensure our remains are handled properly. Shortly after that, they must learn to adjust to living without us. No one likes to lose anything, especially a family member or loved one. It's never easy to accept, but life continues on after our friends or family members are gone. Most feel the shock at some point, and some people choose to deny their beloved one's departure happened and go on living as if their loved one's death never occurred. For example, when my mother passed away, how I dealt with the situation was to tell myself my mother was on an extended vacation. I asked God to show me where she was, and He showed me a vision of her in heaven playing and singing with children. They were all holding hands in a circle of love. This was such a lovely vision because my mother had been robbed of her childhood. She was raped at a young age. I believe that whatever you suffer on earth, God restores back to you in His kingdom. In this vision, my mother was surrounded by children in a beautiful meadow. It appeared to be a bright and sunny day, and her face was full of light. After seeing this, I was at peace and grateful that my mom was finally complete and whole and in a place where bad memories and schizophrenia didn't exist. Telling myself she was in a happy place, as well as seeing the vision, helped me process through the pain, until I could accept her departure.

Everyone deals with loss differently, and it is important to deal with it and not cover up the pain. I have read numerous articles about the stages of loss. One stage is denial, as I just mentioned, followed by shock, guilt, depression, hope, acceptance, and anger (please note, these don't come in perfect order). When my son passed away, all I could think about was how cheated I felt. Whose fault was it really? I would shake my fist in the air and ask why he did such a stupid thing when he was so young, loved, admired, and so very talented. I fought that anger every day. I would give it to God, then the next day, I would take it back and ponder over the reasons why I thought he took his life. I would have thoughts about the people that had let him down and such, and this stage was the beginning of the blame game, which is part of what is called bargaining. You ask yourself what you could have done to prevent this calamity and who was really responsible.

This stage was the beginning of a vicious cycle of overthinking the event and going over every detail. Along with this came the wild rumors; one of them was my son was murdered. Of course, emotions ran high during this time as I tried to fit the pieces together, but by the grace of God, we made it through this very rough time. At the end of it all, I just believed he took his own life and that my son's bad decision was just something we all eventually had to accept and live with for the rest of our lives.

The main thing was to adjust to the reality that my baby boy was gone and it was real, and nothing else mattered. What did it matter if he was murdered? We couldn't bring him back. And this statement wasn't meant to be disrespectful in any way to those who have lost loved ones through the act of murder or accidents or even the subject matter of suicide, because the pain is real and it's a tragedy, but blaming and holding grudges will only delay your healing. I made a conscious decision to forgive him or the possible person who could have taken his life.

At this point, I began to practice forgiveness, repeating prayers that would bring peace and healing. My prayers were similar to what Jesus had prayed when He was set up by religious leaders and so-called followers of truth. They belittled and shamed Him, then finally killed Him. But Jesus, knowing the secret of being set free is forgiveness, said these words before His departure: "Father, forgive them, for they don't know what they are doing" (Luke 23:34, NLT). And the soldiers gambled for His clothes by throwing dice. Imagine Jesus hanging on a wooden cross, with nails in hands and feet, on public display, seemingly helpless and in excruciating pain, His jaw swollen and probably almost toothless, bleeding profusely. He could barely even utter words because of His condition, and He was forced to listen to soldiers mocking Him and gambling like it was a joke. They had just crucified a holy and innocent man. How much more did they have to do to display their hatred? When you think about this, you should ask yourself what your excuse is for holding on to grudges. In this prayer I modeled after the Savior, it covered everyone: the possible murderer and suicide tragedy. When all of these things occur, it's up to you and me to release the pain to a higher power; otherwise, we walk around in circles going nowhere. It is certainly a process that must be worked out by letting go of the past, because you can't change it anyway, and beginning to grow and forgive. It takes practice; it just doesn't happen. It's an intention you have to set, and the faster you activate it, the faster you move forward. Otherwise, you'll do a constant repeat of, "Just what could I have done to save my loved one? How could I have stopped this calamity from occurring?" When you think of those who could have been involved, such as the possible person who may have killed him, you torment yourself and say, "We should have been paying closer attention to the details."

As difficult as it all was and still is (but it's easier to cope now), I make a conscious choice every day to remain in forgiveness. I take control over my thoughts. What helps me do this is meditating on scriptures, so as these feelings of unforgiveness pop up, I resist them with scriptures like this one: "Set your minds on things above, not on earthly things" (Col.

3:2). Earthy things are the lusts and temptations that usually get us all into much turmoil. Unforgiveness is earthy because when people hurt you, you look for a way to get them back or you find an earthy way to fix your pain. I have become stronger because God is healing me. The healing has taken place because of my choice to forgive. No one can make you forgive; it's a choice that will bring remarkable change in you and others (because they see a change in you). It just has to be done, then you will experience inner peace, and as crazy as it may sound, you will have a joy that will begin to carry you. If you read Nehemiah 8:10 (NKJV), the last sentence in the scripture says, "Do not sorrow for the joy of the Lord is your strength." It is so supernatural, it will embrace and keep you from crumbling, and the peace that accompanies this will become your best friend. The kind that is found in Scripture:

> They must turn from evil and do good, they must seek peace and pursue it. (1 Peter 3:11, NLT)

How can you ever have peace if you don't choose to pursue it? Some seem to think it will just naturally occur, and maybe in some cases it does, but most of the time, you have to fight for it. You have to work through the process of negativity and choose to forgive and move on with your life. Allow the Lord to deal with the things and people and circumstances that you have little or no control over anyway. God's peace is supernatural, and it's what you need when your world comes crashing down.

Mental Disorders: The Painful Truth

Mental disorders have plagued my family tree for generations. My mother was schizophrenic. My natural father and my late son, I believe, had undiagnosed manic-depressive disorder. My stepfather, I believe, had undiagnosed schizoid personality disorder (aka just plain ole aloofness). My natural brother had manic depressive disorder/bipolar disorder and was hospitalized for it. The list goes on and on. Actually, quite a few of my immediate family members have spent more than one night in a mental institution as a patient, except me. I've only been a visitor, by the grace of God. The personality disorders I grew up with in my family tree helped shape my way of viewing the world. I learned very early on to make my own reality when I wasn't happy with the way things were going. Writing creatively and listening to music became great escapes from the mental chaos that surrounded me as a child.

Reese's Struggle with Manic Depression

The old classic song "Tears of a Clown" by singer Smokey Robinson is a story about a person who appears happy on the outside but on the inside is crying. My son Reese had a way of making you laugh and perk up if you were feeling down. He did it with such finesse and care; it was like medicine. And even though he appeared joyful and full of life, he had tense moments that made you wish that the certain subject matter at hand had never been discussed or mentioned. He would get stuck in a depressive cycle, and it was as if he had in earplugs and couldn't hear you. He would repeat the negative things he experienced. Every one of us at some time in our lives will be mistreated. It is unfortunate, but being a victim will lead you to the bottom of a false reality so that you can't rise to the top and become a victor! This sort of negative talk only leads to more aggression and anger.

In your anger do not sin; do not let the sun go down while you are still angry. (Ephesians 4:26, NIV)

This was a scripture I kept thinking about after Reese was gone. What we meditate on overtakes us. That's why the Good Book says, "Finally brethren whatsoever things are true, whatsoever things are honest, whatsoever things are just, whatsoever things are pure, whatsoever things are lovely, whatsoever things are of good report, if there be any virtue, and if there be any praise, think on these things" (Phil. 4:8, KJV). I have practiced this, and it works. I wish my child could have practiced this on that dark day, but instead I heard his friends say that he would utter the words, "I'll show everyone that I don't have to be mistreated or disrespected." When I think about this, I'm reminded his home had gotten broken into just before Christmas and a lot of valuables were taken. The feelings of loss and vulnerability were still very fresh in his memory. Furthermore, his main source of income had come to a halt, and he was feeling a sense of loss of control of his life. Those things that were once so close, easy, and familiar were gone, and the pressure of bills was starting to get to him. I recently lost my job after twenty-seven years of the same routine—getting up at the same time every day, taking the same route to and from work, stopping at the same places to shop—and it was a great loss for me. It altered my life in such a way that I didn't know how to live anymore in the first few years. I'm still adjusting, and I must think positively so that I don't let these changes destroy my life. Our lives are worth so much more than the things we've lost.

"These pictures were taken at the very beginning of Mama Roza's illness, showing signs of great depression in the early stages of schizophrenia"

"Mama Roza was in her early twenties".

"Mama and me when I was around 13 months old".

"Mama and me when I was about four years old".

"Mama Roza with friends and family during the holidays".

"Mama and me when I was an infant in front of our home on 7th Avenue in Spokane, Wa.".

Schizophrenia and Mama "Roza"

In the mid-seventies, the movie *Sybil* came out. It was a story about a woman named Shirley Ardell Mason who suffered from mental illness. I was intrigued by this movie because it showed on the big screen a woman who was mentally ill and needed treatment. The movie helped me understand what my mother was going through. Shirley, the main character, was a bright young woman who had abusive parents. Because of the abuse she sustained, and the trauma caused by it, her brain figured out a way to escape it. She ended up with something called DID,[4] which

_____

[4] . Dissociative Identity Disorder.

resulted in sixteen different personalities. It was later determined that she may have faked some of the personalities, but the evidence was clear that she was a tortured soul. After the book and the movie were released, there were multiple cases of this disorder revealed in the United States. My mom didn't have DID; she was diagnosed with schizophrenia. Movies such as *The Soloist* and *A Beautiful Mind* portray main characters with mental illness. *A Beautiful Mind* especially took me back to the dark, gloomy season in my life when my dear mother would go into a state of hallucinations and hear voices in the middle of the night. It always seemed to happen when I was in a deep, sound sleep and usually in the middle of the night between 3 a.m. and 5 a.m. Voices would drift from her bedroom that sounded as if two people were having a conversation because she would pause to listen and answer like a question was being asked.

There was a time I felt frightened and didn't want to sleep in my bed alone, so I jumped in her bed; this seems paradoxical, but she was still my mom and I was looking for comfort. I found the opposite because an incident occurred on this one particular night. She woke me by asking over and over again if I could see the black cats that were crawling on the wall. I was in grade school and had to get up early the next morning, and I didn't sleep well for worrying and wondering what on earth she was talking about. My mother didn't drink, so she wasn't intoxicated; I couldn't understand why she was seeing and hearing all those voices. This was my dilemma all through my childhood years. One early morning, I was awakened by hard knocking on the front door. I jumped out of bed and ran urgently to the door. I asked who it was because I was taught to never open the door for strangers. The voice on the other side of the door identified himself as a highway patrolman, so I opened the door to a pair of compassionate officers. They told me my mother was found walking down the middle of the freeway with a suitcase in her hand with traffic coming toward her. The police picked her up and took her to Medical Lake, a mental hospital. That particular facility was where some of my family members resided until they were mentally stable enough to return back home to their own immediate families.

"Me, around age 2, with my step dad, Frank".

"Frank relaxing at home".

"Frank with guitar".

"Frank and me when I was a toddler".

"a sketch (drawn by Joy Sutton) of my step dad playing his favorite game, chess".

Schizoid (Aloof Personality Disorder): "Frank"

Frank was my stepfather. He took on the responsible role of parenting me from the age of nine months old. My birthplace is in the southern United States. Silence was the code in my family because of the shame of mental disorders and such, so I'm not sure of all the details. However, it's obvious that my natural dad, Bill, aka Vern, was no longer in a harmonious relationship with my mother shortly after my birth. All I knew was my stepfather loved my mom and married her. They were from two different worlds. She was African-American with Brazilian ancestry, according to my grandmother Martha Lee, and my stepfather was Caucasian English. He was a seaman in the navy. The fifties were full of racial tensions, and I assume that could have been their motivation for moving up north to Washington state. I was just an infant and have little knowledge of how they initially met. My stepfather retired from the navy at some point and began his new occupation at St. Luke's Hospital as a superintendent, while my mother pursued her dream as a dress designer. She could make just about anything she laid her eyes on, and her garments were store quality. Back in those days, there was no such thing as online computer courses. If you wanted an education and couldn't go to a traditional brick-and-mortar college, you could take a course by mail.

Frank was a very matter-of-fact kind of guy, very intellectual and aloof. He was hard to get close to but was very reliable and responsible. The rent was never late, the electricity was always on, and we always had food. He interacted very little with me, but he and my mother would sometimes have intellectual talks about politics and war or discuss other subjects way above my comprehension. They would have these discussions while my mother was cutting patterns or drawing designs for her next creation or while he was filling out his chess cards. He was an avid chess player and played with champions in the United States and overseas. He would go to Seattle every so often for tournaments as well. Those with schizoid personality disorders feel more comfortable in relationships that have little or no emotional attachments, so chess was the perfect social pastime for him. It dealt with timing and strategy. Although my stepfather showed little emotion, I knew he loved me, because he would give me instructions on how to save and budget money, and he was also concerned about my physical needs being met. As I grew older and wiser, I realized that he did the best he could to support my needs, but emotionally he just couldn't. With my stepfather's aloofness and my mother's mental challenges, their marriage was a constant merry-go-round, and it left me always feeling uncertain about the future. It's funny how my mom still expected certain things from my stepfather in spite of her schizophrenic tendencies. She was still a woman with emotional needs, and when she felt they weren't being met, they would argue for days on end.

Eventually, I grew up and moved out, but I would visit on occasion to check on them. As time progressed, I noticed my stepdad appeared more withdrawn and stopped playing chess socially. He appeared depressed; he let his hair grow long and ran from the slightest possibility of interaction with other people. But on one particular day when I came to visit, he greeted me in an unusual manner. He answered the door (which was rare), and instead of running to shut himself in his private quarters, he was very inquisitive. He looked me in the eyes and asked, "What happened to you?" At first, I didn't understand what he was talking about, but after a moment, it dawned on me that he must have been paying attention to my slow transformation. I became a born-again Christian. My style of dress changed, and the way I spoke to my parents changed. Forgiveness had entered my heart. The Word of God was coming alive in me, like this verse of Scripture: "A soft answer turneth away wrath: but grievous words stir up anger" (Prov. 15:1, KJV). Yes, this was the modification operating in my heart. I was no longer on the defensive. It was wonderful to have my stepfather become more personable with me. I had always wanted to be closer to him, and now I was seeing the fruits of my prayer labor coming to fruition.

Frank's Battle

It looked like things were turning around in my family. Seeing my stepfather start to show interest in me was a great beginning. On my next visit with him, his unanswered question came up again regarding my change. I was almost insulted, thinking, *Am I really all that bad?* But I refrained from letting my flesh rise in anger and instead began to figure out how I would explain my Christian conversion to this man who doesn't even believe in God. Well, with much prayer for wisdom, the answers began to flow from my mouth. The last thing I wanted to do was clash with him and give him a sermon about how Jesus Christ, whom I love and adore, gave me hope, peace, and joy. I didn't want to argue with him about how he doesn't think God exists, especially since this was the first real time we had ever spoken more than a sentence to one another. As I was praying for wisdom, before my mouth opened, the thought came to me that I should just say it! So I took a deep breath and said boldly, "I've been born again!" He looked at me sideways and said, "What?" I took another deep breath and explained to him that I prayed a simple prayer. I told him my prayer to God was this: "God, I am tired and miserable, and I feel hopeless. If I can't live a happy, functional life, then just take me out of my misery." What I didn't tell my stepfather was that he and my mother had a great deal to do with me asking Jesus into my heart.

Before I explain what happened with Frank, let me explain how I became a born-again Christian. A year prior to my born-again experience, I saw a movie called *The Exorcist*. For some strange reason, my parents thought I should join them on movie night, and when we left the theater, I felt like someone was following me. I kept looking behind me, and the only people that were there were my parents. So I decided to slow down and let them go ahead of me then check to see if I had the same feelings, and I did. This time, when I looked behind me, there was no one there, or at least no one I could see with my eyes. For several days, weeks, and months after, I would hear strange noises near my bed at night. It got to the point that I wasn't sleeping well and was fatigued most of the time. The final straw was when I could physically feel hands pulling me to the window and pushing my body to make me jump. What I didn't realize was that these were the spirits that had plagued the atmosphere of my parent's home, and really the same spirits that were in my family tree my whole life. The deep depression my father was in was giving him suicidal thoughts. After my encounter with these suicidal demons, I knew I needed special help.

When I was eleven, my mother went into a mental institution for the second time. She thought it was best for me to go into a foster home while she was away. As frightened as I was to be separated from my parents, and especially my mother, I didn't resist or run away. I submitted to the state of Washington's social services regulations and was administered a case worker. As a result, I was placed in a Christian home with the honorable Bishop C. E. and Pauline Hamp. As uncomfortable as I was going into foster care, it really turned out to be the best thing that ever happened to me. It saved my life and my soul. I will never forget the day I was driven to that white parsonage house with the large white church directly next door. My heart was pounding as the caseworker and I walked up the long walkway and climbed the stairs to the enormous porch. I stood flat footed as she rang the doorbell. I could hear the footsteps getting closer and closer, then finally the door opened wide and out stepped the tallest man I had ever laid eyes on. I gave him a once-over. I started from his Stacy Adams shoes and worked my way up to the authoritative grin he displayed, and I thought, *Better not mess with him, or he'll let ya really have it!* This new atmosphere was exactly what I needed. With the sanctuary right next door, it was never a hassle getting to church. Youth service was every Friday night, and it was on one of those wonderful nights I gave my heart to my Lord and Savior for the first time. The suicidal thoughts never plagued me again.

But it wasn't until eight years later that I really understood how important my decision was to allow Christ to be the head of my life. My stepfather didn't know that God was using him and my mother to draw me into salvation (because of the movie invitation to watch *The Exorcist*). Sitting there talking to my stepfather, I remained calm and continued my testimony, and for the first time ever, I witnessed his undivided attention. As I looked into his eyes, I could see his weakness and that his will to live was fading. I hadn't realized until this point how serious it was. Having the presence of the Holy Spirit there made this easier for me than I ever could have imagined. I was feeling pretty bold at this point, so I asked the question to this man who I thought was a total non-believer. I said, "Would you like to accept Jesus Christ, the Son of God, into your heart?" His voice broke, his eyes watered, and he reached out his hands and replied, "Yes." And at that moment, he became a believer. I would have one final visit with my stepdad to encourage him and share scriptures. I was looking forward to a great, fulfilling relationship with him as a believer. Instead, I got a phone call about three weeks later from my mother telling me that while she was out of town on a business trip, she had received a call from the hospital where my dad worked telling her she needed to come home immediately because her husband had passed. My stepfather, being such a perfectionist, was never late a day in his life that I knew of. This particular day, he was late reporting to work. The house they were renting was owned by the hospital and next to the hospital near where he worked, so when he was a no-call, no-show, which was very highly unlikely for him, a coworker from the hospital came to the house and found the door ajar, only to behold him swinging by the neck just above the staircase near the front door.

The feeling of gloom came over me, and I felt like I had failed. But in spite of this, the Holy Spirit reminded me that my stepfather had accepted Jesus into his heart. Back in those days, people would say that it was unforgivable to take your life, but somehow, even though many people believed that, especially in churches across the country, I felt a peace beyond my understanding—a grace and a mercy that understood his pain. I felt he was with the Lord.

This is a plea from my heart to those who want to end their life because the pain is so great. Please don't take this easy way out, because no one knows what's really on the other side of suicide but God. Get the necessary help you need to get your life back on track. You can do it. Don't give up hope. Ask God for strength; when you seek Him for it, you will find it, and you'll know then that the spirit world is real. There is a real devil that hates you, and he hates your creator, God. He wants you to end your precious life because you are a force to be reckoned with when you put your trust in the Lord. Satan knows he can't win the battle when you surrender totally to the Lord.

"Bill Vernon, my biological dad, enjoying a great holiday dinner".

"Bill at his home in Spokane, Wa.".

"Bill with my stepmom, Ethel Mae J Vernon, giving me her attention".

"My dad posing near a campground on a sunny day".

Manic Depressive Disorder/Bipolar and My Dad: Bill, AKA Vern

My natural father was almost like a stranger to me. He was someone who would pick me up on weekends; buy me hamburgers, shakes, and fries; and let me drive his shiny new cars through the open dirt roads. He took me shopping and showed me off to all his friends because he was a handsome man with Cuban and African roots and I was his twin, the female version. Whenever we would visit his friends, there was always plenty of food and alcohol around, and the kids had a lot of freedom. We could do as we pleased, and I thought, *This is great!* No rules to follow; just do as you please. I was sure I would love those weekend visits with my dad, and it was entertaining at first. I could drink beer and dance and witness the freedom the other kids had. Some were still in diapers and saying four-letter words. It was a culture shock for me. My mom was somewhat liberal but would frown on my drinking, smoking, and cursing, so I kept my weekend activities a secret from my mother and Frank. After a while, this kind of routine became empty and meaningless, and my self-esteem took a dive on its way to rock bottom. I wanted my dad to love me like fathers do, by protecting me from bad influences and habits. As the weekend parties continued, he had no real interaction with me. Most of the time, he was cracking jokes or getting high with his friends, and the visits just turned into wild drink-a-thons.

Soon I began to witness his severe mood swings. He would go from happy to sad or mellow to mad in just seconds. I was so confused. There is another part of this story. My natural father and stepmother (Ethel Mae) were married for many years. She was a born again believer and a woman of integrity. She was tall and graceful as a swan, and I loved her. She was always very good to me and treated me as her own when I came to visit their home. My father was very good at persuading her and others that he was on the up-and-up. There is a scripture that reads, "Above all, love each other deeply, because love covers over a multitude of sins" (1 Pet. 4:8). This is the verse that best describes my dear stepmom's personality. She had such a forgiving heart. Another scripture that comes to mind in explaining her character would be Matthew 18:21-22: "Then Peter came to Jesus and asked, 'Lord, how many times shall I forgive my brother or sister who sins against me? Up to seven times?' Jesus answered, 'I tell you, not seven times but seventy times seven.'" Her personality was very loving and forgiving, so you can understand how she was blind to my father's behavior. He had a side of himself he showed her which was respectful of my stepmom, and she spoke highly of him. But the dark side he showed only to me and others, as far as I could tell.

Once as a young teenager, I asked my biological mother, Roza, if I could spend the summer with my dad and stepmom because they had the cool house and the fancy cars, and I would have a nice room and would feel normal, or at least I thought I would. She let me go, and I did feel normal for a while. One of my friends had a car, so I would ride with her often. One day, we went to the movies. I had asked permission from my dad to go, and everything seemed fine until I came home early that evening while my stepmom was at work. It was around seven or eight in the evening, not past my curfew. I said hello and proceeded to go to my room, but my father barged into my room and told me to leave. Because he was such a joker, I didn't take him seriously. I just ignored him, turned around, and took the clothes from the middle drawer and laid them at the foot of the bed. Then he yelled again for me to get out and grabbed my arm and began pulling me toward the bedroom door. I lost my balance and hit the floor, and he didn't even look back to see if I was hurt. He dropped my arm and grabbed one of my legs instead and dragged my body like a sack of potatoes to the door, then threw me into the driveway. I was in disbelief. I got up and barged through the door, reentered my room, and shut the door. I could hear his heavy footsteps getting closer to my bedroom door. I stood there praying and hoping that he was just playing a silly joke on me or that maybe he drank a little too much this particular evening and was coming to apologize. But my fantasies of being treated like a normal, privileged teen were about to end pretty quickly. The door opened widely and slammed into the wall, probably leaving a hole in it. He grabbed me once again by the ankle and tossed me into the driveway, but this time, it wasn't so easy to get right back up again because I was breaking on the inside. I didn't have the strength to get back up and go to that beautiful bedroom that was once mine for just a few weeks. It was over. My body began to feel the pain of the toss and struggle. While I lay there sobbing, the door opened once again, and a garbage bag full of my belongings was tossed on top of me like it was Saturday morning trash day. I banged on the door until I got him to open it. I groveled like a beggar asking him to let me please use the phone to call my friend to pick me up, and finally he agreed. But I knew he meant business, so I didn't push his limits. Thank God for my friends. They pulled into the driveway about thirty minutes later. I really had nowhere to go. My mother's mental illness at this time was too much for me to endure. The whole purpose of me living with my dad for the summer was for me to find some normalcy, but instead I got even more madness.

Manic Depression/Bipolar Symptoms

Mania is a surge of energy that lasts for long periods of time, even days, with little sleep. Some people have hallucinations and severe mood swings. This state of mind, as it intensifies, can lead to heightened irritability that can lead to violence, anxiety, and suicidal thoughts. Some individuals become delusional and get so down and depressed that they feel responsible for things happening in the world. Sometimes symptoms overlap and this disorder starts to look a little like schizophrenia.

I have seen these symptoms my whole life, first in my natural dad, then my brother, then finally my son. All three of them tried to self-medicate with alcohol, sex, or drugs. When depression sets in, it's like a cancer. It wants to spread until it consumes you. If you are already struggling with depression, the last thing you need is a drink of alcohol, since alcohol is a depressant. It makes the manic state way worse when consumed. All three of my family members were trying to find peace in a bottle of liquid courage and trying to get strength to get through each day, but this temporary fix just leads you in circles.

Depression Can Lead to Suicide

Controlling your thoughts can be difficult for those who suffer from depression, but it is necessary. Rehearsing negative thoughts produces certain chemicals in your brain to cause your mood to become dark and discouraged. There are certain things and people you should avoid if possible. They will become triggers to set this kind of dark mood in motion. Get yourself to a place of light and enjoyment, and I don't mean drugs or alcohol. If you are on prescription medication for your disorder, make sure you are taking the proper dosage and have a friend or family member you can trust to refer back to about how you are coming along (accountability), because it is very easy to become addicted to prescription drugs. Maybe you have anger outbursts but have never been to a clinic or doctor because you never thought you had a problem. Maybe you do or maybe you don't. But the reason for this book is to get you to take a look at yourself, your friends, and your family members. I'm not just spilling my guts to you to merely tell you about my family's mental conditions. I'm sharing my personal testimony so you can compare your experiences directly or indirectly and to possibly help you find a solution to the turmoil you are facing. No one gets to pick their family members, so if you have mental illness in your family, then you do. You can't change them, but you can change you and become the best you that you can be. Start reading about how to deal with depression and fight your anger and discouragement. The main thing is to never give up on yourself. You deserve to live. Learn to appreciate your uniqueness because there is only one you. Face yourself and live your life.

The work I did to make myself the best me I could be wasn't done alone. I went to counseling, I confided in friends and some family members, and I read plenty of books. But my greatest help was giving all my pain and unanswered questions to the one who understands all situations, the one who never gave up on me, and the one who loves me in spite of all of my mistakes and misfortunes. If you don't know by now who this person is—it's God. His love unlocks the door of the prison life has put you in. I like this scripture found in Acts 16:25-26: "About midnight Paul and Silas were praying and singing hymns to God, and the other prisoners were listening to them. Suddenly there was such a violent earthquake that the foundations of the prison were shaken. At once all the prison doors flew open, and everyone's chains came loose." Worshiping God is the best strategy for easing the burden of the emotional and spiritual baggage that weighs us down. It will loosen the chains and open the doors to the freedom the Lord wants you and me to live in.

Finding Balance

Life has a rhythm to it, and when you're out of sync, it's hard to get back in step because you don't know what to do. Life as you once knew it is gone, and it can be scary and difficult to start anew. But those of you who have family or friends that go through anything like this, just know this is a major life change. Please don't be the kind of friend that just says, "I love you"—be the kind that shows the love by serving your friends and family. You can bring food or money, spend time together, offer to clean, cook, or give a ride, or just show some support by being there. Love is a verb—it needs action. You may be wondering why you should give your hard-earned money, time, or affection. The answer is in one of my favorite songs, "Everything Must Change." Everything but God will surely change, and life is full of uncertainty. No one likes to think about it, but if there was a natural disaster or any circumstance that was beyond your control, the life you once knew would be altered and you would be left trying to pick up the pieces. Remember, just as you plant seeds in your garden to grow fruits and vegetables, you must also plant or invest in others. Again, love must be demonstrated; otherwise, it's a "tinkling brass or sounding symbol" as it says in I Corinthians 13:1 (KJV). You become a person who's just making a lot of noise. We are only people, not gods, but God is in every one of us, like the Lord revealed to me in the revelation I shared in the paragraph with the heading, "Accepting the Unacceptable: A Change of Focus." We may not always feel like loving or sacrificing for our loved ones, but each time we do, you can believe that it brings our Lord pleasure and joy and there is a reward on the other side of the blessing you sowed.

My son loved the Lord and was torn between his music career and its culture and the call that was upon his life, as many of us are. God's grace and mercy found Reese, and I am grateful. I give honor and glory to Him who has set me free and given me the strength and ability to write these words to share with others. You will find your balance. If you had never ridden a bike before or not for a long time, you would have to practice keeping the bike steady so it wouldn't tip over. Eventually, you find that with enough practice, at last, you're on your way down slopes and up hills and around corners just like before, so be patient—you'll find balance again; it just takes practice.

This Victory Is Yours

I used to ask myself why I was born into this family. I used to go to my friend's house and do chores for their parents hoping they would see that I had great potential to be a responsible, loyal, and loving kid. I hoped that they could love me and want to have me around, but it was always short-lived because my friend's parents had their own children to house and feed. Years of being in a toxic household makes you want to break away. It made me want to pursue a normal, structured life. Somehow, I suppose we pass on to our children what's been handed down to us, even if we are the new and improved models, because all of us are somehow a product of our environment. That's why it's so important to be connected to the right kind of people. The only way to find out if they are the right kind of people is to give the relationship a chance.

If you have demonstrated some toxic behavior toward your own children, don't be too prideful to apologize. If you grew up in a cesspool of funk, there's sure to be some residue that remains, but let your goal always be to improve and move forward. Always be regretful for the mistakes you've made but never live in condemnation. When God forgives, He wipes away your sins, but the pain you have caused others may still possibly linger in the minds or hearts of those who have been affected. Please know and understand that they also have a responsibility to let go of past hurts and move forward, just like you. Once you realize this, you won't be so vulnerable and as easily manipulated into carrying the guilt torch (carrying the guilt and shame of past mistakes for all to see and criticize and judge), because Jesus already did that for us all. Please read and live this passage of scripture from Romans 8:1: "Therefore, there is now no condemnation for those who are in Christ Jesus." Generational problems are real. Statistics show that if you were raised a certain way, the habits and mistakes will be passed down to the next generation, but the greater truth is you can change that through prayer and fasting and by making better choices. You don't have to accept that fate. 2 Corinthians 5:17 (KJV) states, "Therefore if any man be in Christ, he is a new creature: old things are passed away; behold all things are become new."

Mental Illness in the Bible?

Most of us who have read the Bible have heard of the man who was a lunatic in Mark 5:1-20.[5] This man would cut himself and scream, and he hung out at a gravesite; no one was able to restrain him because of his enormous strength until he found Jesus. Jesus was the only one who could set him free. When you read this story, you will see that Jesus said to this man, "Come out of this man, you evil spirit." Now to some this may sound a bit harsh, but notice Jesus was referring to the spirit as an

---

[5] . I suggest you read the NIV translation.

evil spirit. Let's lay out the foundation of our human structure. It's three-fold. You have a body, and inside your body is a spirit and a soul. You know what your body functions are—you walk, talk, sleep, eat, think, smell, taste, etc. Maybe you don't understand what your soul's function is. It's your will, intellect, and emotions. Your spirit is how you connect with God, but it must be trained to stay in harmony with Him. You can look at it this way: your cell phone has more than one function. You can call others and others can call you, and you can use it like a computer to write letters, check your messages and emails, etc. However, it's still only one phone. It has many functions and capabilities, but if it's not maintained properly, it won't perform well and will begin to malfunction.

In the gospel of Mark, Jesus had to deal with this man's spirit. There was something evil inside him that had taken over, so Jesus addressed the spirit, not the man. When doctors treat patients for mental disorders, they first diagnose and then come to a conclusion as to how to treat it. The treatment will be twofold. They will prescribe medication for your body, then they will deal with your soul—your emotions, will, and your ability to comprehend reality. That's about as far as it goes in most cases, unless the doctor feels the patient needs spiritual guidance or help and, if so, would suggest a clergyman to assist further. At that point, then the Holy Spirit would give you the guidance you need to live a life of victory when you choose to accept Him. There is nothing like a minister who can offer some hands-on counsel, because most of them are aware of spiritual warfare. When all three of these are properly nourished, you have harmony and balance in your life and a much healthier outlook on life.

Notice how Jesus went straight to the problem that no one else could handle. When it comes to people being tormented with feelings of depression, DID, schizophrenia, schizoid, addictions, or other mental illnesses, remember that Jesus is the ultimate power and solution.

Chapter 13

Medical Definitions of Alcohol and Drugs and the Effects They Have on Your Body and Mental Health

In most dictionaries, you will get the basic definition of what alcohol is. In the Merriam-Webster online dictionary, it describes alcohol as "ethanol especially when considered as the intoxicating agent in fermented and distilled liquors; [or a] drink such as whiskey or beer containing ethanol; [or] a mixture of ethanol and water that is usually 95 percent ethanol."[5] Wikipedia defines alcohol as "any organic compound in which the hydroxyl functional group (-OH) is bound to a saturated carbon atom. The term alcohol originally referred to the primary alcohol ethanol (ethyl alcohol), which is used as a drug and is the main alcohol present in alcoholic beverages."[6]

The definitions are very similar, but if you dig deeper and go to the etymology of the word, you will find alcohol comes from the Arabic Al-kohl, which means "body-eating spirit" and serves as the origin for the English word for ghoul. According to Middle Eastern folklore, a ghoul is an evil demon believed to eat human bodies. This information can be found in several articles written by Auricmedia (The Costa Rican News,[7] Wiktionary).[8] There are many articles on the subject of alcohol. Several articles mention that when a person drinks in excess, they have a memory lapse. It's very typical for people to get drunk and not remember a thing they did or said the next day. I have witnessed this first hand for years working in the casino industry. It's quite common. Also, it's very common for people to demonstrate the Dr. Jekyll and Mr. Hyde effect. Some of the most mild-mannered people turn into the Incredible Hulk after a few shots of tequila. There's more to this than meets the eye. Don't you think it's interesting the nickname for liquor, wine, and beer is spirits? And it has been this way for many years. It's posted on taverns and pubs all over the globe. We see it and probably never take it seriously because it's the antidote or the temporary emotional painkiller. If you enjoy old westerns like I do, you see the doctors used whiskey for surgery preparation, and it was the main painkiller used when removing a bullet. I have read at least half a dozen articles on this Arabic definition. It once was known as a type of powder from which makeup originated for beautification purposes, but these readings went more into detail about how science has discovered that alcohol consumption over long periods of time has been known to cause cancer in males and females.[1] In fact, after a while, men begin to develop feminine physical traits such as breasts and shrunken male organs. So, you see, alcohol is the liquid drug that alters mind, body, and spirit. Go online and read for yourself the side effects they don't want you to know about (the ones that profit from your pain and pleasure). Information is key to making better choices. If you don't have this information, how can you choose better? Places like https://www.cancer.org and https://www.cdc.gov are good places to start.

The Definition and Effects of Marijuana

Marijuana refers to the dried leaves, flowers, stems, and seeds from the hemp plant, Cannabis sativa. The plant contains the mind-altering chemical delta-9 tetrahydrocannabinol (THC) and other related compounds. Extracts can also be made from the cannabis plant. The THC acts on specific brain cell receptors that ordinarily react to natural

THC-like chemicals. These natural chemicals play a role in normal brain development and function. Marijuana over-activates parts of the brain that contain the highest number of these receptors. This causes the "high" that people feel. Other effects include:

- Altered senses (for example, seeing brighter colors)
- Altered sense chime (sounds like a chime ringing)
- Changes in mood
- Impaired body movement
- Difficulty with thinking and problem solving, impaired memory
- Hallucinations (when taken in high doses)
- Delusions (when taken in high doses)
- Psychosis (when taken in high doses)
- Temporary hallucinations
- Temporary paranoia
- Worsening symptoms in patients with schizophrenia—a severe mental disorder with symptoms such as hallucinations, paranoia, and disorganized thinking. Marijuana use has also been linked to other mental health problems such as depression, anxiety, and suicidal thoughts among teens. However, study findings have been mixed.[6]

The Definition and Effects of Heroin

A white crystalline narcotic powder derived from morphine, formerly used as an analgesic and sedative: manufacture and importation of heroin are now controlled by federal law in the United States because of the danger of addiction. A white bitter crystalline compound (Dictionary.com).

---

[6] U.S. Department of Health and Human Services. The National Institute on Drug Abuse (NIDA). [Online; accessed 10-May-2019]. 2019. URL: https://www.drugabuse.gov.

Short-Term Effects

People who use this drug report feeling a "rush" (a surge of pleasure or euphoria). However, there are other common effects, including:

- Dry mouth
- Warm flushing of the skin
- Heavy feeling in the arms and legs
- Nausea and vomiting
- Severe itching
- Clouded mental functioning
- Going "on the nod": a back-and-forth state of being conscious and semiconscious

Long-Term Effects

People who use heroin over a long period of time may develop:

- Insomnia
- Collapsed veins for people who inject the drug[7]
- Damaged tissue inside the nose for people who either sniff or snort it
- Infection of the heart lining and valves
- Abscesses (swollen tissue filled with pus)
- Constipation and stomach cramping
- Liver and kidney disease
- Lung complications including pneumonia
- Irregular menstrual cycles for women
- Mental disorders such as depression and antisocial personality disorder
- Sexual dysfunction for men

---

[7] Needle Injections also carry a higher risk for contracting HIV, hepatitis C, and other blood-borne diseases.

The Definition and Effects of Cocaine

Cocaine is a substance derived from the leaves of the coca plant that is a bitter, addictive substance. This drug is a stimulant and is used in the medical profession for pain and to control bleeding, etc.

Short-Term Effects

Short-term health effects of cocaine:
- Extreme happiness and energy
- Mental alertness
- Hypersensitivity to sight, sound, and touch
- Irritability
- Paranoia—extreme and unreasonable distrust of others

Long-Term Effects

Some long-term health effects of cocaine depend on the method of use and include the following:

Snorting: loss of sense of smell, nosebleeds, frequent runny nose, and problems with swallowing

Consuming by Mouth: severe bowel decay from reduced blood flow

Needle Injection: higher risk for contracting HIV, hepatitis C, and other blood-borne diseases

Crack Cocaine

This is a mixture of cocaine, baking soda, and water. This combination is then cooked on an open flame. After a process, it hardens into a rock that is then smoked. These are the short-term physical and mental effects of smoking crack. They appear to be more intense than the effects of snorting or injecting the drug. The effects of smoking the drug are similar to other commonly abused stimulants, such as methamphetamine.

Because crack is produced in unregulated settings from cocaine and is of inconsistent purity and quality, the precise effects vary greatly, but generally include:

- Euphoric "rush"
- Increased alertness
- Excited state
- Decreased appetite
- Dilated (enlarged) pupils
- Increased heart rate
- Intense craving for another dose shortly after the high subsides

It is said users feel very euphoric or high when using crack. The paradoxical drawbacks are a short-term high with feelings of depression and paranoia. An example of this would be an exaggerated misconception of someone trying to steal from them or harm them, which in turn would lead to aggressive behavior.

Side Effects

These are the commonly reported side effects of using crack:

- Irritability
- Anxiety
- Headache
- Depression
- Aggressive, paranoid behavior
- Abdominal pain
- Sudden death due to heart attack or stroke

Crack addiction came on the scene sometime in the early eighties. Street dealers were facing a drop in drug sales, and the poorer neighborhoods that wanted a quick fix couldn't afford to buy cocaine to snort; so smoking it in rock form became the temporary drug fix. It was cheap and easy to obtain. The epidemic has lasted nearly three decades. Crack is the perfect name for this drug because your life just slips right through the cracks when you use it. People will lie, cheat, steal, and sell themselves (prostitution) and their own babies for the drug (I'm not suggesting that everyone who uses crack has done this). With this form of cocaine, there are more side effects that are unpleasant, such as "crack bugs," etc. I suggest you go to the website drugabuse.com to read the entire report. If a person is already struggling with mental disorders, using any of the drugs I've mentioned (especially street drugs) that haven't been properly measured or tested will only make things worse.

Opioids

DrugAbuse.gov[9] defines opioids as a class of drugs found naturally in poppy plants that include the illegal drug heroin, synthetic opioids such as fentanyl, and pain relievers available legally by prescription, such as oxycodone (Oxycontin) and similar substances. These drugs are primarily used to treat moderate to severe pain, though some are used for treating coughing and diarrhea.

Effects from opioids include:
- Drowsiness
- Confusion
- Nausea
- Constipation
- Euphoria
- Slowed breathing

The real danger comes in the form of its addictiveness. Although most opioids are legal, they have some of the highest addiction rates among any drug, rivaling caffeine.

In Conclusion

have shared with you my own supernatural experiences, as well as deep secrets from my early childhood and adulthood. Some of these experiences were shameful and uncomfortable; some were beautiful and breathtaking. I began to document all these events and discovered that this was a healthy way to process the hurt, anger, and fear I was feeling, and it has helped me find answers. Searching for answers is an important part of getting well. You may not get every question answered, and some may take longer than others to find, but it is important that you don't lie to yourself about where you have come from and where you are now. If you are honest, life won't overwhelm you and send you to places you never wanted to go. My purpose for this book is for you to recognize the toxic behavior patterns in your family and/or in yourself so you can start the process of coping and hopefully stop unhealthy behavior patterns that could become fatal. Once a life is taken, the damage is done. We can't change anyone, but we can help change occur by sharing knowledge with others and praying that the people we have enlightened will now make better choices. I want to thank you for reading my book, and I'm looking forward to meeting some of you at upcoming events. I pray you have many years of success, fulfillment, and happiness. May you grow from victim to victor. God bless you!

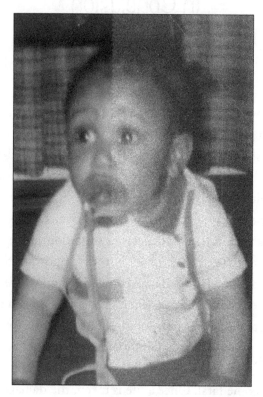

Maurice "Reese" Moncrease
October 24, 1981—January 19, 2013

Appendix A

Biblical Resources

Below is a list of biblical resources, often free, for you to do your own studying, as well as research the verses listed in this book for yourself.

Bible Gateway is a free-to-use compendium of Bibles in a variety of languages and formats.[8] Some good English versions to help you get started are NIV,[9] NASB,[10] ESV,[11] NLT,[12] KJV,[13] and NKJV,[14] and ASV.[15]

Another good, easy-to-find Bible is the Gideon Bible, the gold one often included with hotel and motel rooms.

---

[8]   BibleGateway.com: A searchable online Bible in over 150 versions and 50 languages. 2019. https://biblegateway.com/.

[9]   "New International Version (NIV)–Version Information–BibleGateway.com". BibleGateway. com: A searchable online Bible in over 150 versions and 50 languages. 2019. https:// biblegateway.com/versions/New-International-Version-NIV-Bible/.

[10] "New American Standard Bible (NASB)–Version Information–BibleGateway.com". BibleGateway.com: A searchable online Bible in over 150 versions and 50 languages. 2019. https://biblegateway.com/versions/American-Standard-Bible-NASB-Bible/.

[11] "English Standard Version (ESV)–Version Information–BibleGateway.com". BibleGateway. com: A searchable online Bible in over 150 versions and 50 languages. 2019. https:// biblegateway.com/versions/English-Standard-Version-ESV-Bible/.

[12] "New Living Translation (NLT)–Version Information–BibleGateway.com". BibleGateway. com: A searchable online Bible in over 150 versions and 50 languages. 2019. https:// biblegateway.com/versions/New-Living-Translation-NLT-Bible/.

[13] "King James Version (KJV)–Version Information–BibleGateway.com". BibleGateway. com: A searchable online Bible in over 150 versions and 50 languages. 2019. https://www. biblegateway.com/versions/King-James-Version-KJV-Bible/.

[14] "New King James Version (NKJV)–Version Information–BibleGateway.com". BibleGateway. com: A searchable online Bible in over 150 versions and 50 languages. 2019. https://www. biblegateway.com/versions/New-King-James-Version-NKJV-Bible/.

[15] "American Standard Version (ASV)–Version Information–BibleGateway.com". BibleGateway.com: A searchable online Bible in over 150 versions and 50 languages. 2019. https://biblegateway.com/versions/American-Standard-Version-ASV-Bible/.

References

"Alcohol." Wikipedia: The Free Encyclopedia. 2019.

https://en.wikipedia.org/w/index.
php?title=Alcohol&oldid=890118937.

"Alcohol." Wiktionary: The Free Dictionary. 2019.

https://en.wiktionary.org/w/index.
php?title=alcohol&oldid=52401486.

American Heritage® Dictionary of the English Language. Fifth Edition. Boston:Houghton Mif-

flin Harcourt Publishing Company, 2016.

J Andrew Armour and Jeffrey L Ardell. *Neurocardiology.* New York:Oxford University Press, USA, 1994.

Mitchell G. Bard. *Israel Environment & Nature: Owl.* [Online; accessed 7-May-2019].

Jan. 2016. URL: https://jewishvirtuallibrary.org/owl.

"Definition of Alcohol by Merriam-Webster." Merriam-Webster. 2019. https://www.merriam-

webster.com/dictionary/alcohol.

"Evil." Wikipedia: The Free Encyclopedia.

https://simple.wikipedia.org/w/index.
php?title=Evil&oldid=6251430.

"National Institute on Drug Abuse." The National Institute on Drug Abuse (NIDA). 2019.

https://www.drugabuse.gov

Suicide Prevention Hotline: 1-800-273-8255

TCRN Staff. "The Spiritual Consequences of Alcohol Consumption." 2017.

https://thecostaricanews.com/spiritual-consequences-alcohol-consumption/.